From The Library of
Steve Bishop

For since in the wisdom of God the world through its wisdom
did not know him, God was pleased through the foolishness
of what was preached to save those who believe. Jews demand
miraculous signs and Greeks look for wisdom, but
we preach Christ crucified;
a stumbling block to Jews and foolishness to Gentiles, but
to those whom God has called, both Jews and Greeks, Christ
the power of God and the wisdom of God.

I Corinthians 1:21-24

We ✝ Preach Christ Crucified

Sermons in
honor of
Frank Pack
by his
students

Edited by Jerry Rushford

PEPPERDINE UNIVERSITY PRESS
Malibu, California

Library of Congress Cataloging in Publication Data
Main entry under title:
We preach Christ crucified.

   Contents: Sermons in honor of Frank Pack, Distinguished Professor of Religion at Pepperdine University, by 25 of his former students.
   1. Churches of Christ—Sermons.   2.Sermons, American.
3. Pack, Frank,1916-   I. Pack, Frank, 1916-
II. Rushford, Jerry, 1942-
BX6799.C26A48   1986   252'066   86-5066
ISBN 0-932612-14-8

Dedication
To the former students of Frank Pack
who now proclaim Christ throughout the world

ACKNOWLEDGMENTS

I would like to express my appreciation to Brenda Zobrist for her editorial assistance, to Helen Kilday for typing the manuscript, to Bill Henegar for the dust jacket and book design, to Bill Roberts for the art and printing production, and to Dean Zarr for helping us reach our publication deadline.

CONTENTS

Committed to New Testament Christianity

A PROFILE OF FRANK PACK

In *Who's Who in America* for 1984-85, Dr. Frank Pack is quoted as saying: "From my youth I have been committed to New Testament Christianity. This faith I have shared with others. By Christ's standards I have endeavored to live and to serve."

One of the most powerful influences in the background of Frank Pack occurred years before he was born. It was the day his mother, Mary Gibson, heard T. B. Larimore preach the gospel of Christ near her home in northern Alabama. The impact of that sermon remained with her the rest of her life. After Mary had married Walter Pack and moved to Memphis, Tennessee, she looked for a church where the preaching would be like that of Larimore. She visited the Church of Christ that was meeting on Harbert Avenue, and when she heard John Allen Hudson preach, she knew she had found a home.

When the Harbert Avenue congregation moved into its spacious new building on Union Avenue in 1925, Walter and Mary Pack became more involved in the life of the church. N. B. Hardeman was called to preach in a gospel meeting at Union Avenue in the summer of 1926, and during the course of the meeting, Walter and Mary Pack were baptized into Christ.

The four years that John Allen Hudson preached in Memphis were pivotal for young Frank Pack, for it was during those years that the seed was planted. Several months after the baptism of his parents, during a gospel meeting preached by Horace Busby, 10-year-old Frank was baptized into Christ. He already knew that he wanted to preach. In fact, he had known it for some time.

Frank's keen intellect began to manifest itself in his early youth as he graduated from grammar school as valedictorian and from high school as salutatorian. During those years, he was nurtured by the preaching he heard at Union Avenue. John Allen Hudson was followed by C. A. Norred in 1926 and by G. C. Brewer in 1929. Among the preachers who frequently filled in at Union Avenue when Brewer was traveling were J. N. Armstrong, L. L. Brigance, A. G. Freed, and N. B. Hardeman. As Frank listened to Brewer and Hardeman, he was hearing two of the most powerful preachers in the church of that day.

In the summer of 1932, Frank moved to his grandparents' home in Nashville as he made preparation to enter David Lipscomb College in the fall. He was eager to begin preaching, and the opportunity was not long in coming. He preached his first sermon before the Reid Avenue congregation in Nashville on July 10, 1932. He was just 16 years old. Twenty-five years later, he returned to Nashville to preach again at Reid Avenue on the silver anniversary of his first sermon.

In his three years at Lipscomb (1932-1935), Frank preached somewhere nearly every Sunday. He took courses in church history from the president, Batsell Baxter, and courses in philosophy from the dean, E. H. Ijams. Along with fellow students like Howard A. White, M. Norvel Young, Batsell Barrett Baxter, Willard Collins, and Jim Bill McInteer, he took courses in Old Testament from Dr. Hall L. Calhoun and courses in New Testament from R. C. Bell. The courses on preaching and the life and work of the minister were taught by H. Leo Boles and Charles R. Brewer. During these college years, Frank became a close friend of the young preacher for the Hillsboro Church of Christ in Nashville whose name was J. P. Sanders.

Perhaps the most powerful influence on Frank's development as a preacher was the time he spent listening to Dr. Hall L. Calhoun, his Old Testament professor and the preacher for the Central Church of Christ in Nashville. Calhoun was an outstanding scholar who had studied under the legendary J. W. McGarvey at the College of the Bible and had completed a Ph.D. in Old Testament at Harvard University.

In addition to his work with the Central Church and his teaching responsibilities at Lipscomb, Calhoun preached daily over radio station WLAC in Nashville.

The three student years that Frank spent in Nashville were the last three years of Calhoun's life, but they were also years in which Calhoun was at the peak of his powers. "His greatest work was done in the last years of his life," Frank remembers. Frank often visited in the home of the scholar-preacher, and the example of Calhoun would serve as a role model for the young teenager for many years to come.

In 1935, Frank returned to Memphis and remained for the entire summer. With G. C. Brewer traveling across the country conducting evangelistic meetings, the Union Avenue congregation asked their young college student to do all of the preaching. At the age of 19, he preached for three consecutive months for one of the largest and most influential churches in Tennessee.

The next chapter in Frank's life took him to Chattanooga where he preached for the St. Elmo Church of Christ and completed his B.A. degree at the University of Chattanooga. The church allowed him to spend much of 1938-39 in Nashville so that he could study toward his M.A. degree at Vanderbilt University, and that degree was conferred in June, 1939.

Later that summer, Frank Pack and J. P. Sanders finalized plans to travel to Scotland for a year of graduate work at the University of Edinburgh under teachers such as John Baillie. They had already booked passage on the Queen Mary when the storm clouds of war in Europe forced them to cancel their plans. Frank spent one more year with the St. Elmo church before accepting the offer of a position on the Bible faculty at David Lipscomb College.

When Frank arrived at Lipscomb in the fall of 1940, it marked the beginning of a remarkable teaching career which has now spanned forty-six years. The Grace Avenue Church of Christ called him to be their preacher, and for the next four wartime years, Frank divided his work between the college and the church. Near the close of that time he began to make plans to return to school and enter a doctoral program. It was Batsell Baxter who urged Frank to consider the University of Southern California for his advanced studies.

For the last six months of 1944, Frank devoted his time to preaching in numerous gospel meetings across the country as he prepared to make the move to California. He arrived in Los Angeles in February, 1945, and enrolled immediately at USC. By September of that year, he was also teaching for George Pepperdine College and preaching for the Burbank Church of Christ.

It was in the pulpit at the Burbank Church one Sunday morning in August, 1946, that Della Carlton first saw Frank Pack. She was visiting at the invitation of the George Beal family, who were members of the congregation. Della was immediately impressed with the 29-year-old preacher, and he was certainly not oblivious to her presence. She stayed for the pot-luck dinner following worship, and afterwards Frank drove her home. They were constant companions in the next few months, and they announced their engagement in December.

Della was a Kansas native who had attended college in Oklahoma and had moved to California to complete her degree at USC. She was teaching school in San Marino and was a member of the Central Church of Christ in Los Angeles when she first met Frank. They were married on June 22, 1947, at the Vermont Avenue Church of Christ adjacent to the Pepperdine campus in Los Angeles. Dr. W. B. West, Jr., chairman of the Bible department at Pepperdine, performed the ceremony.

Frank was awarded the Ph.D. in New Testament in 1948, and by 1949 *Dr.* Pack had accepted the invitation of President Don H. Morris to join the Bible faculty at Abilene Christian College in Abilene, Texas. Starting in 1952, Della was also a member of the ACC faculty, teaching courses in elementary education.

The move to Abilene was the beginning of a significant chapter in Frank's career in which he influenced hundreds of young preachers who came to ACC for their training. He continued to preach during these years, serving both the Northside and Graham Street congregations in Abilene for several years each.

One of the young men who studied under Dr. Pack in those Abilene years was John Gipson. In a recent letter to his former teacher, John wrote:

> There is no way I can repay the debt which I owe to you. I marvel at your knowledge and insight, the matchless manner in which you preach, and especially the goodness I find in your life. No young preacher could desire a better model or pattern. Your love of truth, your understanding of the human heart, your joy in living, your patience with immature students, your constant encouragement, your love of family, your

> sense of humor, live before me every day and shout
> Christ! You have been, and are, one of the greatest
> blessings of my life.
>
> There is simply no way to tell of the impact you have
> made for good on hundreds of us who endeavor to
> preach. Over the years I have asked countless preachers
> the question, "Who was your favorite teacher in
> school?" Invariably the answer is "Frank Pack." No one
> ever accused you of being "easy," but they were ready
> to admit that you were the best!

After fourteen years of faithful service to the students of Abilene Christian College, Frank and Della answered the urgent call of President M. Norvel Young to return to Pepperdine College in Los Angeles. For four months in the fall of 1963, they were privileged to travel around the world. At the beginning of January, 1964, they were back home in the city of their marriage.

For the past twenty-two years, Frank has preached for the Culver-Palms Church of Christ in Los Angeles and has served on the faculty of Pepperdine University. In addition to teaching, he was chairman of the Bible department from 1964 to 1972, and again from 1980 to 1983. He also served as Dean of the Graduate School from 1967 until 1978. Dr. Pack was promoted to Distinguished Professor of Religion in 1978. Della was a member of the Pepperdine faculty from 1964 to 1977.

Frank Pack has now been preaching for nearly fifty-four years. His teaching career at three Christian colleges spans forty-six years. During these same years he has preached in more than 300 gospel meetings and has been a featured speaker in college lectureships throughout the nation. Not content to confine his efforts to the pulpit and the classroom, Frank has also been a prolific writer. He has published nine books and more than 300 articles in his productive career.

This commemorative volume is timed to coincide with two significant events in Dr. Pack's career: his seventieth birthday on March 27, 1986, and his retirement from full-time teaching at the close of the summer session in 1986.

When the idea for this book occurred to me in the summer of 1985, I asked Dr. Pack at lunch one day if he knew how many of his former students were still faithfully at work preaching the gospel. Although he couldn't give me a number at that time, he indicated that he would look back through all his class roll books and provide me with a list of names. Several weeks went by, and then one day, Dr. Pack presented me with a typed list of more than 500 names of his former students who were currently preaching or teaching Bible in a Christian college. I think we were both surprised at how many names were on the list.

All the sermons in this book were preached to the glory of God. They were contributed to this special anniversary volume, still to the glory of God, who gave us Frank Pack. Each of the contributors has devoted much of his life to preaching the gospel of Christ, and each is a former student of Frank Pack. Following is a brief word about each man:

Dan Anders preaches for the University Church of Christ in Malibu, California.

Michael Armour was president of Columbia Christian College in Portland, Oregon, from 1982 to 1986. He now preaches for the Skillman Avenue Church of Christ in Dallas, Texas.

Tony Ash is a professor of Bible at Abilene Christian University in Abilene, Texas, and he preaches for the 11th & Willis Church of Christ in Abilene.

Joe Barnett preached for the Broadway Church of Christ in Lubbock, Texas, from 1968 to 1980, and is now president of Pathway Evangelism, a nonprofit organization focusing on media ministries.

Bob Barnhill preaches for the Harpeth Hills Church of Christ in Nashville, Tennessee.

Gayle Crowe preaches for the Chatham Church of Christ in Chatham, New Jersey.

Ken Dye preaches for the Broadway Church of Christ in Lubbock, Texas.

Geoffrey Ellis preaches for the Waterloo Church of Christ in Waterloo, Ontario, Canada.

Paul Faulkner is a professor of Bible and director of the Marriage and Family Institute at Abilene Christian University. He preaches frequently throughout the country.

John Gipson preaches for the 6th & Izard Church of Christ in Little Rock, Arkansas.

Lanny Henninger preaches for the University Avenue Church of Christ in Austin, Texas.

Charles Hodge preaches for the Duncanville Church of Christ in Duncanville, Texas.

Jimmy Jividen preached for the Alameda Church of Christ in Norman, Oklahoma, from 1981 to 1985 and has taken two years off to write two books.

Steven Lemley is president of Lubbock Christian College in Lubbock, Texas, and he preaches frequently throughout the Southwest.

Bill Love preaches for the Bering Drive Church of Christ in Houston, Texas.

Avon Malone is an associate professor of Bible at Oklahoma Christian College in Oklahoma City, and he preaches frequently throughout the Southwest.

Dick Marcear preaches for the Central Church of Christ in Amarillo, Texas.

Randy Mayeux preaches for the 37th & Atlantic Church of Christ in Long Beach, California.

Howard Norton preached for the College Church of Christ in Oklahoma City, Oklahoma, from 1983 to 1986, and he will become chairman of the Bible department at Oklahoma Christian College in the summer of 1986.

Harvey Porter preaches for the Montgomery Boulevard Church of Christ in Albuquerque, New Mexico.

Joe Schubert preached for the Bammel Road Church of Christ in Houston, Texas, from 1973 to 1983, and he is now president of the Center for Church Growth in Houston.

Silas Shotwell preaches for the South Painter Avenue Church of Christ in Whittier, California.

David Tarbet preaches for the Danbury Church of Christ in Danbury, Connecticut.

Will Ed Warren is an associate professor of Bible at Harding University in Searcy, Arkansas, and he preaches for the Sheridan Church of Christ in Sheridan, Arkansas.

William Young preaches for the Alta Mesa Church of Christ in Fort Worth, Texas.

Each of the men who contributed to this volume feels a sense of great indebtedness to Frank Pack. Bill Love spoke for all twenty-five when he wrote in a recent letter to Dr. Pack:

> It's hard for me to believe it has been twenty-five years
> since I sat with others in your "Revelation" class in the

new south wing of the Ad building! Professors seldom
know how profoundly they affect their students. That
study of Revelation has been a strong anchor for my
developing faith and theology ever since. I hope the
sermon enclosed will be a respectable benchmark of
that continuing quest and will, in some small way, bring
much-deserved honor to you. God has blessed, and
will richly bless, so many of us through your ministry!

The welcome news is that Dr. Pack has agreed to continue teaching
on a part-time basis at Pepperdine University. As he enters his eighth
decade, he still serves the Culver-Palms Church on a regular basis. New
books and articles are in preparation. The indefatigable ministry of the
scholar-preacher continues. This brief volume is our way of expressing
gratitude for the first seventy years of the one who said: "From my youth
I have been committed to New Testament Christianity. This faith I have
shared with others. By Christ's standards I have endeavored to live and
to serve."

Jerry Rushford
Malibu, California
March 27, 1986
Frank Pack's 70th Birthday

A PICTORIAL CHRONOLOGY

Frank at age six with younger brother

Frank was salutatorian and city
debate champion at Memphis
Technical High School

Union Avenue Church of Christ, Memphis, Tennessee

Reid Avenue Church of Christ,
Nashville, Tennessee

FRANK PACK
MEMPHIS, TENNESSEE

We never knew so young a boy with so old a head.

Preacher's Club; Winner, Founder's Day Medal, '33.

From the 1934 David Lipscomb College Yearbook

The young preacher in 1938

St. Elmo Church of Christ, Chattanooga, Tennessee

THE PEPPERDINE YEARS 1945 - 1949

Burbank Church of Christ, Burbank, California

Wedding Day—June 22, 1947

Frank and Della in 1947

THE PEPPERDINE YEARS 1945 · 1949

The Pepperdine religion faculty with Ernest Colwell, president of the University of Chicago, and Edgar J. Goodspeed, noted Bible translator. (l to r) Billy Yount, Joseph White, Frank Pack, W.B. West, Jr., Colwell, Goodspeed, Ralph Wilburn, L.D. Webb, and Morgan Harlan.

The Pepperdine religion faculty. (seated l to r) Frank Pack, Ralph Wilburn, W.B. West, Jr., Joseph White, and Morgan Harlan. (Standing l to r) J. Eddie Weems, J. Herman Campbell, Hubert Derrick, Russel Squire, and Wade Ruby.

THE ABILENE YEARS 1949 - 1963

THE PEPPERDINE YEARS 1964 -

The new chairman of the religion department with Howard Horton in 1964.

The New Dean of the Graduate School in 1967.

Receiving Pepperdine's Christian Service Award from President M. Norvel Young.

*Culver-Palms Church of Christ,
Los Angeles, California*

*Visiting lecturer at South
Africa Bible School in
Benomi, South Africa in
1971.*

*The Culver-Palms Church
facetiously gave Frank a director's
chair when he completed the
filming of his lectures on the gospel
of John in 1982.*

*Frank in 1982, portraying
Barton W. Stone at the 150th
anniversary celebration of the
merger of the Stone and
Campbell movements.*

Frank and Della in 1985

1

Affirmation

JOE BARNETT

After Henry Ward Beecher had become an internationally famous preacher, he stood in his Brooklyn pulpit one day and attributed his achievements to a woman who taught for one term in the rural school he attended as a boy. Through understanding and skill, he said, she had started him in the right direction. She had seen something in him and believed in him. That day, standing before his congregation, he tearfully said, "I have forgotten her name."

I

Most of us have such persons in our background. Those who have studied people of achievement invariably point to one common ingredient—there was someone who believed in them and encouraged the best in them. A mother or father. A teacher. A friend. Someone.

I remember Mrs. Womack. She was my first-grade Sunday School teacher. I don't remember how she looked. Or how old she was. In fact, I remember very little about her. But I remember that she gave me a lot of attention; she apparently believed in me, and unselfishly gave of herself to teach me and make me feel important.

I don't remember any of my other Sunday School teachers until I was in junior high school. Then, there was Vance Mitchell. The elders asked him to take the junior high boys' class. He protested that he'd never taught; he didn't know how. They said, "We don't care if you teach — we just want you to control those boys. Bring some order out of the chaos." He accepted the challenge. He was big enough to demand order, and did when he had to. But he didn't have to do much of that. He got us to do things we would never have dreamed of doing. For instance, he got us to memorize all the cases of conversion in Acts. And, somehow, it was fun. Vance Mitchell took an interest in every boy in that class. He learned a lot about each of us. His contact was not limited to Sunday morning. He came by to see us. He called us on the phone. He believed in us. And he got the best out of us.

When I was in high school, the elders asked some of us to make talks on Wednesday night. Clarence Nelson, one of those elders, came to me after my talk and said, "Joe, I hope you'll be a preacher. You have what it takes. Think about it." Every time he saw me he encouraged me.

Affirmation! We all need it.

II

The most gripping illustration of this I've seen lately comes from Dr. Stanley Mooneyham. Dr. Mooneyham was chief executive officer of World Vision from 1969 to 1982. He has probably had more to do with feeding the world's starving than any other person.

He recently told of an encounter he had when he was 10 years old which still impacts his life.

Mooneyham was born in the rural deep South several years before the Depression. He was the seventh and last child of a tenant farmer who could hardly write his name. He wore hand-me-down clothes, took biscuits and fried sweet potatoes to school in a little pail for lunch, and stood with his mother in food lines for government handouts to poor families.

This early and intimate association with poverty had a terrible effect on him. He developed a devastating inferiority complex. It was so overpowering that he dreaded facing each sunrise. For protection he withdrew into himself. This created an emotional paralysis which produced a speech stammer so severe that he couldn't answer any questions orally in class. He had to write his answers on the chalkboard.

Sometime during this black period of his life, Mrs. Beasley, a wonderful grandmother-type lady who was County Superintendent of Schools, took an interest in him for some reason. Occasionally she would send word to his teacher to have W.S. (that was what they called Stan) come by her office in the County Court House after school. All day he would savor the anticipation of spending a few minutes with this person of such obvious value and worth. He says that on those days he always felt better about himself, though he couldn't have told you why.

Usually Mrs. Beasley would give Stan a book that had just arrived from the publisher and trust it to him for a few days with the words, "I think you'll enjoy this." That Mrs. Beasley even thought about him was wonderfully affirming. That she would trust him with a brand new book made him feel 10 feet tall.

Since his severe stammer made oral communication almost impossible, he by necessity took up writing. At age 10 he started to write the great American novel. One day he found the courage to show Mrs. Beasley the first five pages. She gushed. "W.S.," she said, "you are going to be a writer." And she said it with conviction. "I just know it! This is good! Now, you keep on writing, you hear? I want to put your books on my shelf."

Well, Stan never wrote the great American novel. And Mrs. Beasley didn't live long enough to have any of his other books on her shelf. But the thing that kept him writing through a shower of rejection slips from publishers that would paper your living room wall was that Mrs. Beasley told him he was a writer. And even if the editors and publishers didn't recognize it, Mrs. Beasley knew. She believed in him.

Since then Stan Mooneyham has had his share of manuscripts published, and he testifies that every one of them is a tribute to a woman who believed in a little boy who was too shy to believe in himself.

III

Now, consider Jesus' treatment of a woman caught in the act of adultery. In the eyes of the legalistic Pharisees she was the lowest form of human life, deserving death by stoning.

Their judgment probably confirmed her feelings about herself. She was already filled with shame, burdened by guilt, and crushed by self-loathing. No one had to tell her that sexual promiscuity failed to live up to its advanced billing as a fun-filled evening. Her sin had left her empty and guilt-ridden. She knew she was less than she could be, less than she wanted to be.

That's true with most of us. We know our weaknesses, our sins. Like this adulterous woman who was already agonizingly aware of her defects, we don't need the verdict of "guilty" repeated over and over again. We need an announcement of grace. We need someone to believe in us. We need love and affirmation. Most often what we get — and what we give — is judgment and condemnation, and nearly always with disastrous results.

George Bernard Shaw, in one of his plays, said, "It is easy, terribly easy, to shake a man's faith in himself." To take advantage of that to break a person's spirit is devil's work.

A psychologist tells about a woman who came to him for counseling. In her mid-30s, she was stunningly beautiful. But her marriage was in crisis. She found it impossible to freely give herself to her husband, she said, because she was so ugly. The psychologist, who rated her a perfect "10," thought she was jesting, until in therapy her feelings about her perceived ugliness emerged. As a teenager her face was marked by recurring acne. She wore thick-lens glasses and had shiny braces on her teeth.

Walking across the campus one day she heard an upper-class boy comment, "She wouldn't be bad if you put a bag over her head." This judgment, delivered by one of the most popular boys in school, devastated her. From that day on she considered herself ugly. Twenty years later her teeth were straight, the acne was gone, and contact lenses had replaced the heavy spectacles. The ugly duckling had metamorphosed into a beautiful swan in everyone's eyes but her own. Her psychologist said she was still looking for an appropriate bag in which to hide her head.

Our words are powerful. No wonder James spoke of the dual nature of the tongue this way: "With the tongue we praise our Lord and Father, and with it we curse men, who have been made in God's likeness."

In one case, words of encouragement and affirmation gave hope to a shy country boy. And in the other, a thoughtless put-down kept a young girl from ever knowing how beautiful she really was.

What a wonderful example of unconditional acceptance and affirmation Jesus provides. He is the ultimate affirmer, accepting the misfits and outcasts, the imperfect and blemished. The only people Jesus put down were those who put others down. He had no sympathy for the self-righteous Pharisees whose stock-in-trade was enhancing their own religious image by highlighting the defects of others.

When they brought the woman to Jesus they were met by withering silence, except for his invitation that anyone without sin was permitted to cast the first stone. When her accusers crawled away, Jesus affirmed her worth as a person, without endorsing her lifestyle. When he told her, "Neither do I condemn you, go and sin no more," it was the ultimate affirmation which must have rekindled within her some sense of value as a person and as an offspring of God. It had to be a profound and life-changing experience.

Look at the tax collector, Zacchaeus, hated and ostracized by the entire community. This little man must have grown immensely in self-esteem as a result of the acknowledgment of his worth by Jesus. Knowing how much Zacchaeus needed to be affirmed, not condemned as a social outcast, Jesus invited himself to a meal with Him. That Jesus thought him worthwhile enough to spend time with him was overwhelming. He now had a value to live up to, instead of a sleazy past to live down. I believe it was this affirmation which prompted him to volunteer to repay, with 300 percent interest, all those he had cheated. He even offered to give away half his money to the poor.

IV

I have come more and more to believe that affirmation of worth is a far more powerful motivator to good than judgment and condemnation can ever be. Jesus told people they had value, that He believed in them, that they could be all they yearned to be. And, with but few exceptions, they strained every spiritual muscle to prove him right.

Even when He was rejected He continued to love. A rich young ruler came to Him asking the way to life and happiness. Jesus told him it was not only in keeping the commandments — which he had done without satisfaction — but in making a total commitment. The young man wasn't yet ready to go that far, so he turned to walk away. Mark records these tender words, "And Jesus beholding him, loved him." Even in rejection there was the affirmation of love. I somehow believe the young man was never able to forget that.

Recently there was a memorial service for a well-known business leader. In the subdued atmosphere of mourning, various friends offered their tributes. Near the end, a young black man stood. The other speakers had been controlled and eloquent. But this young man, under great emotional stress, could barely speak. He struggled for words.

With tears streaming down his face, he told the gathering that when he was just an office boy this man had noticed him, helped him, encouraged him. He had even paid for his education. "For a long time," he said, "I was no good to him or anyone else. I just failed and kept on failing. But he never gave up on me, and he never let me give up on myself."

He went on to say that anyone can support a success, but only a rare and wonderful person can continue to have faith in a failure.

Affirmation! What a beautiful thing.

V

In a university setting "people balance" is difficult to achieve. Academic ethics demand quality. It is immoral to claim academic excellence while sending graduates out into the world unprepared to compete in their chosen profession.

Still there is a place in every setting, university included, for genuine feeling, for an interest in the person of the student.

I've never had a teacher who better achieved that balance than Dr. Frank Pack. He holds academic excellence in great respect, and he is highly regarded by his peers for his own academic achievement. And he expects the best from his students.

But he also has genuine feeling for each student. Each of us can relate our own personal encounters with him — encounters which have been warm and affirming.

We all take a bit of justifiable pride in having sat at his feet. We still go back now and again to the notes we took in his classes. And I, for one, invariably find my mind wandering past the notes to the man. He gave us knowledge and developed our skills. More importantly, he pointed us in the right direction.

Awhile back, a successful businessman sat in a preacher's office, discouraged and dejected. He said he had spent his entire professional life climbing the ladder of success, only to discover when he reached the top of the ladder that it was leaning against the wrong wall.

Direction is terribly important. Dr. Pack has helped thousands of us to lean the ladder against the right wall.

He believed in us.

He affirmed us.

He helped us fall in love with Jesus.

2

The Unseen Hand

BOB BARNHILL

Roger is a member of the church. He has been since youth. He was reared in a Christian home. At the age of 13 he was baptized. As Roger looks back on his life, he sees happy memories of some of the great gospel preachers of the past who held meetings where he attended. When he reached adulthood, Roger became interested in the cottage-meeting filmstrip series. Consequently, he was able to baptize a number of his friends. He is married to a fine Christian woman. They have several children. Roger never misses a service. In spite of this creditable heritage, Roger seems to be an individual who lacks something in his life. You see, Roger believes that for all practical purposes, God is not near to him! Basically, Roger feels that God worked in the affairs of men throughout the Old and New Testament periods but that at the cessation of miracles God "lifted" Himself from the scene and is now in heaven. Prayers to Roger are long-distance telephone calls to God. To him, God is not near.

This isn't an idle exaggeration. Churches of Christ today are filled with "Rogers." Somehow in our efforts to avoid obviously unbiblical teachings such as tongue speaking and "divine healing," we have swung to the opposite extreme. We've concluded that God is not active in the affairs of men today! To us, God published His book and left — only to return someday to collect the royalties.

The Bible addresses itself often to the subject of the providence of God. It teaches that God — even in the 20th century — is still active in the affairs of men. His behind-the-scenes direction of affairs was clear throughout the Old Testament in nations, individuals, and circumstances. Paul declared in Galatians 4:4, "In the fullness of time," Jesus came to the world. The Savior's appearance was prefaced by the advanced preparation of nations, individuals, and circumstances, so that Jesus' arrival had maximum impact. God's unseen hand prepared the "fullness of time"! Speaking to a group of pagans, Paul referred to God's guidance of the affairs of men as, "In Him we live, and move, and have our very being" (Acts 17:28). That is how involved God is in our lives.

Literally, providence means "guidance, planning, and forethought behind the scenes." Unlike bold, miraculous intervention (which was so prevalent in Old and New Testament times), the providence of God has always been subtle. The very nature of providence implies it is never distinctly revealed.

I strongly suspect this is precisely why providence is never discussed. We can't see it! It's vague, and we can never be absolutely "sure." Our heritage in the church demands that we be precise and sure about everything. The Bible is hazy on the "how" God providentially works in our lives. In Psalm 40:5 David explained, "Many O God, are thy wonderful works which thou hast done . . . they can't be reckoned up in order unto thee . . . they are more than can be numbered." The apostle Paul could not always tell for certain that events were influenced by the hand of God guiding and directing lives. As he wrote to Philemon (in Philemon 15), he explains the runaway slave, Onesimus, may have escaped from his owner for God's purposes. "Perhaps he departed for a while that ye should receive him forever." In all likelihood, God is vague — on purpose! He keeps His options open. After all, not knowing "how much" God intervenes keeps us busy doing all that we can to determine our own destiny!

Another reason that we may not have preached on providence is our lack of experience. To see the hand of God working in a person's life requires years of living. For one to be able to look back and conclude with a reasonable certainty that "God may well have worked out events in our life for a good purpose" takes some time. Only after Paul had preached for many years did he mentally recall his past life and say things had happened . . . for the furtherance of the gospel" (Philippians 1:12). It was only after many difficult trials that Joseph could look back and declare that his ordeal was used by God for the good (Genesis 50). David declared, "I have been young, and now I am old, and I've never seen the righteous forsaken, nor His seed begging bread" (Psalm 37:25). Earlier, as a shepherd lad, David wasn't equipped for his observation! Time has to pass before a person can see God's providence at work.

Pulpits have remained silent on God's providence. By remaining silent we are omitting one of the greatest privileges a Christian has — the privilege of knowing God is our constant strength and helper! God's supernatural direction behind the scenes still exists! The scriptures that affirm this fact are abundant. For instance, God gives power to civil officials (John 19:10, Romans 13:1-21). The powers that be are ordained of God.

God hints at His intervention and work with His followers as a "potter working with clay" (Romans 9:20-11). We are not so "moldable" that we cannot shape our own destinies. The "clay" can mar in the potter's hand! Yet the very fact the Bible speaks of God working with us as "clay" shows that He works in our lives. His unseen hand is trying to guide. This work is separate and apart from the word, James emphasized (4:15). "If the Lord wills, we will do this or that" — indicating that the Lord has something in mind for what we do. The days of men performing miracles have ceased, but God is still alive and active.

Here is a crucial point: If God does not work through providence today, prayers are absolutely valueless! Answering prayers requires power and action on God's part. We are told to pray for such things as healings, wisdom, prosperity, and help in time of need. Jesus requires prayer-oriented disciples. He expects us to "ask, seek, and knock" (Matthew 7:7). Asking, seeking, and knocking, according to the Savior, is to be directly rewarded by God through "receiving, finding, and opening." In a commendable zeal to honor the written word, we may, paradoxically, find ourselves praying for God to answer prayers and then denying He does so except "through scriptures." God does not answer prayer merely through autosuggestion!

God has supplied His Holy Spirit to help us, indirectly and supernaturally today. This may play a part in God's unseen guidance. God's indwelling Spirit is present in the Christian (Acts 2:38, I Corinthians 6:19). The Spirit helps us in our weaknesses and assists our prayers (Romans 8:26). Like providence, the Spirit is not something that's "felt." We know He's there by faith. Galatians 3:14 says, "We receive the promise of the Spirit by faith." We know he is there in the same way we have remission of sins; "by faith" we believe it. We don't feel His presence. We know He's there because He says He is there and we believe Him.

Whatever direction God or His Spirit gives is always controlled by the word of God. Even in miraculous times when God intervened providentially in the conversions of the Eunuch (Acts 8:29) and Cornelius (Acts 11:12), the word was used as the power of salvation (Romans 1:16) to those people. This written word wears no halo. Like providence, it appears to be ordinary words on a page. It is printed and read like any other book; yet the word possesses the power to mold and guide a soul.

The providence of God can give us some very wonderful blessings. In the first place, it provides us a sure guide throughout our life. "And we know that to them that love the Lord all things work together for good" (Romans 8:28). The wise man, Solomon, declared (Proverbs 3:6), "In all thy ways acknowledge Him, and He will direct thy paths." God does not assure us that all things will work for our physical good. Many things will not. Sometimes the branches on God's vine have to be "purged" so they will bring forth more fruit. One has only to examine the life of the apostle Paul to see that being a Christian can bring all sorts of adversity. The assurance of God's providence, however, causes the Christian to realize that no matter how much adversity comes into his life, it will ultimately work out for his spiritual betterment someday. This feeling (that God is on our side and will always work things out for our spiritual salvation) is a feeling we have too long neglected. The Christian needs to see — he is never alone!

In the second place, providence will give us a sense of God-nearness. The apostle Paul seems to have sensed God's presence and aid in everything he did. Paul spoke to the Corinthians and told them he would come "If the Lord wills" (1 Corinthians 4:19), and he would stay "If the Lord permits." In a design to strip our religion of anything we can't neatly understand, many a Christian in the 20th century is missing a great privilege of sensing God's nearness and guidance.

The comfort and assurance that comes by knowing God's providence always is directing our lives is something we should never cast aside. Without it man is doomed to a man-centered, work-oriented system of religious bondage. Why are you here today? Why do you have the job that you have? What events in your life caused you to be an individual who cares enough to worship the Lord this morning instead of staying home and sleeping in?

As the years pass and we look back on events in our lives, it doesn't require clairvoyance to feel reasonably sure some of the crossroads we took in our journey have been for the good! "Who knowest whether thou art come to the kingdom for such a time as this?" (Esther 4:14) is a question for every person.

We cannot be sure exactly how much God intervenes. We cannot be sure precisely when God intervenes. But, we can be certain He does intervene! We are what we are today, in part, because of God's providence.

Realizing the role of providence in our lives helps us to appreciate a number of the passages in the Bible which are rich with assurance. With His unseen hand in mind, they come alive for the first time. "Though I walk through the valley of the shadow of death, I will fear no evil, for Thou art with me" (Psalms 23). "The Lord will not forsake His saints" (Psalm 37:28). "Cast all your care on Him, for He cares for you" (1 Peter 5:7).

The Lord worked for you yesterday. He is working for you today. God's providence even works on into eternity. As Paul explained, "Eye hath not seen, nor ear heard of the things that God has prepared for those who love Him" (1 Corinthians 2:9). God be praised for His unseen hand!

3

The Attitude of Jesus Toward Self

HOWARD NORTON

We need to develop the attitude of Jesus toward self. When I say that we need to develop the attitude of Jesus toward self, I want to emphasize that I am not saying that we need to think of ourselves exactly as Jesus thought of Himself. He knew He was the Son of God, and He knew that He was the Lord of the universe. He knew also that He was the Son of Man, and He knew that He was the Messiah. These are attitudes that He had about Himself. To have thoughts such as these about ourselves would be a delusion.

It is His attitude toward the concept of self that we so desperately need. When you look at Jesus and see Him thinking about self as a concept, how did He think? What value did He put on self? If He were here today talking to us, what would He say about the way we should feel toward self?

There is a great deal of emphasis today on self and self-fulfillment. One psychologist, Paul Vitz, has written a book entitled *Psychology as Religion: The Cult of Self-Worship* in which he says that the worship of self is a characteristic of our age. Within this worship of self, we learn that we should do what is best for ourselves. We are encouraged to find ourselves, to feel good about ourselves, regardless of the pain this inflicts on others. We have been told that we should put self first, take care of self, and make sure that self gets first consideration. Once self is elevated to its proper position, we can then do some things for other people if we want to.

I believe that this philosophy, so prevalent in our world, is false. I want us to look at Jesus' attitude toward the concept of self and see how He viewed the subject. Then, I want us to see what we can do to have the same attitude toward self that the Lord Jesus had.

The Life of Jesus

In Acts 10:34-43, the apostle Peter preaches a very brief sermon on the life of Jesus. Some scholars have said that this passage is really a condensed version of the gospel of Mark, and it does appear that way. Here is what Luke records:

> And Peter opened his mouth and said: 'Truly, I perceive that God shows no partiality, but in every nation anyone who fears Him and does what is right is acceptable to Him. You know the word which He said to Israel, preaching good news of peace by Jesus Christ (He is Lord of all), the word which was proclaimed throughout all Judea, beginning from Galilee after the baptism which John preached: How God anointed Jesus of Nazareth with the Holy Spirit and with power; how He went about doing good and healing all that were oppressed by the devil, for God was with Him. And we are witnesses to all that He did both in the country of the Jews and in Jerusalem. They put Him to death by hanging Him on a tree; but God raised Him on the third day and made Him manifest; not to all the people but to us who were chosen by God as witnesses, who ate and drank with Him after He rose from the dead. And He commanded us to preach to the people and to testify that He is the one ordained by God to be judge of the living and the dead. To Him all the prophets bear witness that everyone who believes in Him receives forgiveness of sins through His name' (RSV).

There we have something like a *Reader's Digest* version of the entire gospel of Mark. Jesus lived about 33 years. Many of us are considerably older than Jesus was when He died. How much He was able to cram into 33 short years! The Scriptures say that He "went about doing good." The Scriptures say that He was killed by being placed on a tree and crucified. They say that He was raised from the dead and that He appeared to certain people who had been ordained to be witnesses of His resurrection. The Scriptures say that Jesus has been chosen to be judge of the living and the dead. Here in just a few words we have a panoramic view of the life of Jesus the Lord.

An Interpretation of Jesus' Life

The question is, What is the meaning of this life? What does this life tell us, for example, about self-concept?

Fortunately, the Holy Spirit empowered the apostles to interpret and record the significance of the life of Jesus. They explain to us Christ's attitude toward the subject of self. Three passages tell the story.

"For Christ Did Not Please Himself"

The first passage is Romans 15:1-3. "We who are strong ought to bear with the failings of the weak, and not please ourselves; let each of us please his neighbor for his good, to edify him. For Christ did not please Himself; but, as it is written, 'The reproaches of those who reproached thee fell on me.'" The most shocking thing about this passage is in verse 3: "For Christ did not please Himself." And the apostle tells us this is the way we should live.

"Ridiculous," modern man says. It does appear ridiculous to our age because it goes contrary to almost everything that we hear or read in today's world. So many messages tell us that, above everything else, we should please ourselves. But the attitude of Jesus was completely contrary to this contemporary wisdom. The Scriptures say, "Let each of us please his neighbor for his good, to edify him." So, who comes first here? My *self* or my neighbor? I myself come second. My neighbor comes first. And why is it that Paul lays this burden upon us by the inspiration of the Holy Spirit? Why are we told that what is good for the neighbor comes before what is good for us? Because that was the attitude of Jesus, I must be an imitator of His attitudes. The attitude of Jesus was one of not pleasing Himself. He did what was good for others. He did what was good for the weak; and in the process of doing that, He gave His own life.

Now, we love to know people who put others first, don't we? We have recently lost two beloved brothers in this congregation. Aren't we glad that we knew Al Neel, and aren't we glad that we knew Freeman McKee? Everything I know about these men indicates that they were men who put self way down the list, and they put others first. Do you know why they did that? Because they were imitators of Jesus Christ. That's the attitude He had, and it's the attitude all of us must seek to develop.

"For Your Sake He Became Poor"

Let us look at a second passage about Jesus in II Corinthians 8:9. Paul says, "For you know the grace of Lord Jesus Christ, that though He was rich, yet for your sake He became poor, so that by His poverty you might become rich." Isn't that an incredible verse — that Jesus, who was rich, became poor so that we might become rich? And that is the attitude every one of us needs concerning each other and concerning all of the people who live around us. This selfless philosophy of Jesus, however, flies in the face of today's wisdom.

I wonder what our own attitude would be if a son in medical school were to come home and say, "Dad, I've got something to tell you. I've been thinking a lot about what I'm going to do with my life. You know, you and I have talked a great deal about the medical profession. We've talked about some of the exciting things that I can do with the money I'll earn. But I've been thinking seriously, Dad; and I've decided that once I get this medical degree, I'm going to move to the South Sea Islands, move into a colony of lepers, and serve those people for the rest of my life." What would our fatherly response be? Why, we could think of a thousand reasons why our son should not make such a horrible decision to waste himself and his talent.

There was, however, a Catholic priest in the nineteenth century named Damien who learned about a leper colony in the South Sea Islands. He said to himself, "That's where I want to serve." Over the protests of his superiors, he moved to the South Sea Islands, went into a colony of lepers, washed their infected feet and hands, eventually contracted the disease himself and died a leper. He became poor for the sake of others.

In the 1950s, five young men were massacred in Ecuador in an effort to preach the gospel as they understood it to the Auca Indians. Few people understand why they paid such a price to reach a savage tribe until they read these words in a diary kept by one of the young men who died. "God, Himself, set the pattern, and if He did not hold back His own Son, why should we hold back our own little lives for the sake of security? We are, and must always be expendable." In their deaths, they demonstrated the attitude of Jesus who was rich, yet became poor, that others might become rich.

That is the way Jesus lived, and this is the way He expects us to live. Nothing less than this attitude toward self measures up to God's high standards.

A very dear missionary friend of mine received a call from his wealthy father. The father said, "Son, we've talked before about my business. I've got to do something with it because I can't continue to run it. I want to give you one more chance to come home, take over this business, and run it."

The young man replied, "Dad, I appreciate your offer. I love you and I am grateful for the way you have provided for me. I have decided, though, that I want to give my whole life and all of my energies to preaching the gospel of Christ." My young missionary friend turned down the opportunity to become a millionaire. He became poor that he might help others become spiritually rich. Here is an imitation in real life of the attitude of Jesus toward self.

"He Became Obedient Unto Death"

There is one other passage in Philippians 2:3-11 that I want us to study. This is one of my favorite Bible passages and it says as much about Jesus' attitude toward self as any other single text I know.

> Do nothing from selfishness or conceit, but in humility
> count others better than yourselves. Let each of you
> look not only to his own interests, but also to the
> interests of others. Have this mind among yourselves,
> which is yours in Christ Jesus, who, though He was
> in the form of God, did not count equality with God
> a thing to be grasped, but emptied Himself, taking the
> form of a servant, being born in the likeness of men.

> And being found in human form He humbled Himself
> and became obedient unto death, even death on a cross
> (RSV).

Jesus was a person who did not look just to His own interests, but to the interests of others. He was a person who did nothing from selfishness or conceit. He was a person who counted others better than Himself. And this is exactly what God asks us to do.

How do we develop this attitude of Jesus toward self? It is not easy; and frankly, I have a long way to go before I reach the selflessness that Jesus demonstrated in His life or death.

In Matthew 16:24, Jesus says to His disciples, "If any man would come after me, let him deny himself and take up his cross and follow me. For whoever would save his life will lose it, and whoever loses his life for my sake will find it. For what will it profit a man, if he gains the whole world and forfeits his life? Or what shall a man give in return for his life? If any would come after me let him deny himself and take up his cross and follow me."

Harold Lindsell, the editor of *The Harper Study Bible*, says in a footnote that what Jesus is asking me to give up here is not a group of things. He is not asking me to give up meat during Lent. He is not asking me to give up one of the automobiles I have. He is not asking me to give up things so much as he is asking me to give up me!

Jesus is also asking you to give up self. He is not asking so much for what you own, but for your very being. He is asking you to deny the idea that self is all-important. He urges you to accept the fact that true selfhood happens when you use your life as an instrument for the high and holy purpose of serving God and man.

Paul expressed what happens when Jesus' concept of self is at work in the life of a disciple. "I have been crucified with Christ; it is no longer I who live, but Christ who lives in me" (Galatians 2:20). Self must die with Christ in order to live with Him.

Or, as Dietrich Bonhoeffer, the German theologian who died at the hands of the Nazis said, "When Christ calls a man, He bids him come and die."

4

Fasting and Prayer

DICK MARCEAR

Jesus healed a boy the apostles had been unable to cure. "They asked the Lord, 'Why could we not cast him out?' . . . 'this kind goeth not out but by prayer and fasting' " (Matthew 17:19, 21).

Prayer and fasting is a practice unknown to many Christians. Most Christians pray, but few fast. But, in the Scriptures these two were often linked together. For example:

1. Esther faced a critical situation in her life and in the life of the Jewish people. She was seemingly the only one who could talk with the king about the letter that had been sent authorizing the complete annihilation of the Jews. But, she knew that it was unlawful to approach the king unless summoned. However, she was determined to try it anyway. So, how did she prepare for this pivotal confrontation? Listen to Esther 4:15-16, "Then Esther sent this reply to Mordecai: 'Go, gather all the Jews together who are in Susa, and fast for me . . . I and my maids will fast as you do. When this is done, I will go to the king, even though it is against the law. And if I perish, I perish.' "

2. At the time of Jesus' presentation at the Temple (on the eighth day) we are introduced to an old woman named Anna. Luke said, "She never left the temple but worshiped night and day, fasting and praying" (Luke 2:37).

3. When the first elders were appointed in the churches by Paul and Barnabas the process included fasting and prayer. "Paul and Barnabas appointed elders for them in each church, and with prayer and fasting, committed them to the Lord . . ." (Acts 14:23).

4. Before the church in Antioch sent out Paul and Barnabas on their first mission, they fasted and prayed. "So after they had fasted and prayed, they placed their hands on them and sent them off " (Acts 13:3).

What is fasting?

1. The most common meaning is going without food, but still taking liquids, especially fruit juices.

2. Sometimes a short fast involved abstaining from both food and drink.

What is the purpose of fasting?

1. David Lipscomb said, "The object of fasting was to give spiritual strength in times of weakness, temptation, and trial."

2. "Fasting does not change God," said Kenneth Haggin, ". . . will change you."

3. Fasting is a way to help you draw close to God and center your spiritual focus.

Fasting has had a "bad press"

1. Some have thought:

A. If you fast for three days you'll starve. (Probably not so in America where 70 percent of our dogs are overweight.)

B. Fasting will destroy your health, i.e., tear down body tissue. In response, Dr. Allan Cott, author of the book *Fasting: The Ultimate Diet*, said there are many benefits to fasting. It will help ". . . to lose weight, to feel better physically and mentally, to save money, to lower blood pressure and cholesterol levels, to improve sleep, to cut down on smoking and drinking, to relieve tension, to feel euphoric, to save time, and to slow down the aging process." It almost makes you want to fast even if there was not any spiritual value.

2. Others have thought that fasting was going without food for 40 days and nights. This was done, but very rarely, in the Bible and it always involved the supernatural. There were three biblical examples of a 40-day fast — and note they were not done under ordinary circumstances:

A. Moses (Exodus 34:28). While Moses was in the very presence of God, he fasted. Evidently in God's presence food and drink were not very important.

B. Elijah (I Kings 19:7-8). Elijah made it 40 days, but he had been fed by an angel. Certainly this was not an everyday happening.

C. Jesus (Matthew 4:2). Jesus was led by the Spirit. This is the only record in the gospels of Jesus ever fasting.

The Old Testament and Fasting

1. Only one day of fasting was required, the Day of Atonement (Leviticus 16:29-34; 23:27). The term used to describe this fast was, "deny yourselves" (Leviticus 16:31, NIV), "humble your souls" (NASV), "afflict your souls" (KJV). This fast on the Day of Atonement was referred to by Paul in Acts 27:9.

2. Other fasts were spontaneous, not required by the law. For example:

A. 2 Samuel 7:6 — Samuel told the people if they were serious about returning to God they should fast and seek God in prayer. It was a way to concentrate all their minds on God and to seek Him with all their hearts.

B. Ezra 8:21-23 — When preparing to lead the people from Babylon to Jerusalem they prepared for the journey with prayer and fasting.

C. Daniel 9:3 — Realizing the prophecy of Jeremiah 29:10 that the captivity would last 70 years was almost fulfilled, Daniel prayed and fasted for a spiritual revival among the people. He wanted them to be able to return.

The New Testament and Fasting

1. Matthew 6:16-18. Notice in this context that just like He had said earlier about prayer (v. 5, ". . . when you pray . . ."), He said, "When you fast . . ." (not "if" but "when"). The Pharisees received His condemnation because they did it to be seen of men. He said, "They have received their reward in full."

2. Luke 5:33-35. The question asked Jesus was, "John's disciples often fast and pray . . . but yours go on eating and drinking . . ." Note that they not only prayed but fasted. What's the reason your disciples do not fast? He said it was like having the bridegroom with them, but when He left, "in those days they will fast."

3. There is no church in the New Testament that was ever instructed to fast. Nor is there any example of a church being involved in an "all-church fast."

Summary and Suggestions

1. Fasting is not a command. It would not be right to set up rules and regulations for the church today and say, "Thus saith the Lord . . . you must fast . . ."

2. If you do fast, don't tell anybody. The worst thing you could do is to announce to people what you are doing. If you do, then you have fallen into the snare that trapped the Pharisees (Matthew 6:16-18).

3. Fasting is profitable only if you spend the time saved in study and prayer. Richard J. Foster in his best-seller, *Celebration of Discipline*, said in the chapter on fasting, "It is sobering to realize that the very first statement Jesus made about fasting dealt with the question of motive (Matthew 6:16-18)." In quoting John Wesley, Foster noted, "First let it (fasting) be done unto the Lord with our eye singly fixed on Him. Let our intention herein be this, and this alone, to glorify our Father which is in heaven . . ."

4. The Jews had four fasts following the return from the exile (Zechariah 8:15). In Jesus' day they fasted twice a week (Luke 18:12). Foster noted: "A frequent practice of the Pharisees was to fast on Mondays and Thursdays because those were market days and so there would be bigger audiences to see and admire their piety."

The Didache urged Christians to fast on Wednesdays and Fridays. On Wednesdays they were reminded of the betrayal and on Fridays of Jesus' death.

Romans 14:5-6 seems to center in on whether people should enforce this practice on others or not. Paul said, "One man considers one day more sacred than another; another considers every day alike. Each one should be fully convinced in his own mind. He who regards one day as special does so to the Lord . . ." The days of fasting must come from a man's desire to serve God and not from a regulation set up by some brother.

5. Fasting may be a way for you to center your life on God. If it can be used to help you, then I think you are very wise to fast. But, make sure the reason you are doing so is to focus on God and His will for your life. In Psalm 103:1, David said, ". . . all my inmost being, praises His holy name." God desires for us to seek Him with all our hearts. Maybe joining fasting with our prayers can help.

5

Who Cares for the Children?

LANNY HENNINGER

At that time the disciples came to Jesus, saying, "Who is the greatest in the kingdom of heaven?" And calling to Him a child, He put him in the midst of them, and said, "Truly, I say to you, unless you turn and become like children, you will never enter the kingdom of heaven. Whoever humbles himself like this child, he is the greatest in the kingdom of heaven. Whoever receives one such child in my name receives me; but whoever causes one of these little ones who believe in me to sin, it would be better for him to have a great millstone fastened round his neck and to be drowned in the depth of the sea" (Matthew 18:1-6).

I

In one of his novels, the great Russian author Fyodor Dostoevsky makes one of his characters describe how she would paint a portrait of Christ. Jesus, she said, would be gazing off into the distance, a faraway expression on His face, musing over thoughts "as great as the whole world." One of His hands would be resting on the head of a bright child. The youngster, earnest and innocent, would be looking up at Jesus, peering intently as only a child can. That is how this portrait would be painted; perhaps it is Dostoevsky's own vision of the man from Nazareth. The entire scene is not difficult for us to imagine.

They made it a point to bring their children to Him. Whether friend, kinsman, or stranger. Nameless and faceless, we can see them still, carrying their children to this uncommon man in order that He might touch them, bless them (see Matthew 19:13; Mark 10:13, 16). There came a moment when Jesus' disciples grew curious about the kingdom of heaven. Not about its nature, but about its ranking system: "Who is the greatest . . .?" Jesus answered with a child:
And calling to Him a child, He put him in the midst of them, and said, 'Truly, I say to you, unless you turn and become like children, you will never enter the kingdom of heaven. Whoever humbles himself like this child, he is the greatest in the kingdom . . .' (Matthew 18:2-4).

The sound of His gentle, warm invitation still echoes along the corridors of our memory: "Let the little children come to me, and do not hinder them . . ." (Matthew 19:14). As we read along, the message grows ever more difficult to miss; the writers of the New Testament did not intend for us to miss it. Jesus, "very God of very God," the Word which became flesh, likes and welcomes children. That image is burned deep into the heart of His church . . .

II

But not everyone likes children. Surely you've noticed. W. C. Fields, it is often reported, was fond of saying: "Any man who hates dogs and babies can't be all bad." Even the Lord's disciples, though exposed to His radiant affection for them, found children a nuisance, an irritant, an interruption to the true business of the kingdom (Matthew 19:13). Admittedly, children can be a real bother. They have a habit of getting under foot and in the way. Beyond all that, they are a colossal pain in the heart. Only a parent can understand something of David's terrible grief when he cried out over his lost rebellious son:
"O my son Absalom, my son, my son Absalom! Would I had died instead of you, O Absalom, my son, my son." (2 Samuel 18:33)

But that is not all. There is more. Much more. Listen:
"Whoever receives one such child in my name receives me; but whoever causes one of these little ones who believe in me to sin, it would be better for him to have a great millstone fastened round his neck and to be drowned in the depth of the sea." (Matthew 18:5, 6)

Perhaps Jesus was thinking of young children, young in years. Innocent. Trusting. Vulnerable. Perhaps He had also in mind those who were new to faith, those just beginning to follow after Him. Is it only my imagination, or is there a whiteness at the corners of his mouth, a sternness—scarcely suppressed—as He speaks? Is there in the background of these words some incident, an experience from His past which He had never been able to put out of His mind, that rushes unbidden to the surface now? "Whoever deceives a little one of mine, whoever seduces and harms him, whoever leads him into the darkness, it is far better for that person to be hurled into the sea!"

III

It's a terrible thing to lead another human being into the darkness. What could be worse than to mislead a friend? What is more despicable than to trade on someone's trust, someone's innocence? The rabbis came to regard Jeroboam as the worst of sinners. Not because he sinned (everyone does), but because he led Israel into sin (1 Kings 14:16). Another line from the Old Testament also chills the blood: Ahaziah "walked in the ways of the house of Ahab, for his mother was his counselor in doing wickedly" (2 Chronicles 22:3). It is a terrible thing to lead another person into the darkness.

There are so many ways to mislead a child, so many ways to make him stumble . . .

. . . Sometimes we are cold, unfeeling, hard of heart. Hilarion, an Egyptian who lived at the beginning of the Christian era, wrote to his wife, advising her to rear their expected child if it was a boy. But if it was a girl, she should be allowed to die. "Whoever causes one of these little ones to stumble . . ."

. . . Sometimes we are so preoccupied, distracted, neglectful (this is true with home, school, government, church) that the child finally falls. The haunting lyrics of Harry Chapin's "Cat's in the Cradle" traces the all-too-common experience of squandering life's most precious times until time runs out. "Whoever causes one of these little ones to stumble..."

. . . Sometimes we are deliberate, mean-spirited, cruel beyond words. Our modern generation has developed an entire arsenal of weapons with which to hurt the children: abortion on demand . . . child abuse . . . pornography . . . juvenile prostitution . . . the illusory paradise of drugs. "Whoever causes one of these little ones to stumble . . ."

And what is the justification for this reprehensible harm to the children? What is its rationale, its basis? If we listen we can hear its defense summed up in a single, solitary, grievously misunderstood word: *liberty*. Under the guise of personal freedom, seemingly powerless before the prevailing moral code, fearful of any absolute except the belief that there are no absolutes, our nation pushes on through increasingly troubled waters, a great ship that is all sail but no rudder. We have at our disposal vast amounts of knowledge and technology, but no sense of direction, no heart and soul. Spurred on by greed and the profit motive, men of low mind and dingy morals ply their seedy trade to the cries of a liberated age: "I am free! I am free!" All the while a whole culture, deceived and deceiving, unable or unwilling to intervene, looks the other way. All along the roadside the little ones whom Jesus loves, at the hard mercy of the secular, litter the right-of-way, discarded for the sake of our "freedom" like yesterday's newspaper. "Temptations are sure to come," said the Son of Man, "but woe to him by whom they come!" (Luke 17:1).

IV

Who will care for the children? Of course, the home will. Or at least it should. There is a world of wisdom packed into these old words:

> Children, obey your parents in the Lord, for this is right. "Honor your father and mother" (this is the first commandment with a promise), "that it may be well with you and that you may live long on the earth." Fathers, do not provoke your children to anger, but bring them up in the discipline and instruction of the Lord (Ephesians 6:1-4).

As most of us have discovered, it is easier to quote these words than to practice them. It's one thing to extol the value of a good home and quite another to cultivate those qualities which make it good. One thinks of understanding, compassion, discipline, tolerance, and the precious gift of time; these are among the ingredients of a home, and no one needs to be a genius to know that they are hard to come by. Who will care for the children? The family will.

But who else? Are there not others who will speak for those who cannot speak, who will act for those without power? Who indeed will care for the children, if not the church, the people of faith, men and women of conscience and courage. The church remembers that God makes Himself known to us as "Father," and calls us all into His family. The church remembers that its Lord came to earth as a child. The church remembers Jesus' teaching that unless we become as children the eternal kingdom will not be ours. The church is one place in a world of confusing, conflicting places which comes to the aid of the poor, the powerless, the children. Wherever human dignity and life are on the line, there will God's people be. If we are sometimes less than this, mute and insensitive, preoccupied with our own agendas, politically skilled but lacking the common touch, then it is demonstrated how far we have fallen from our Lord's example and how far we have yet to travel.

Ours is a fragmented, warring age. We are divided over many issues. Above all the questions which polarize people, driving wedges between persons, is the towering image of the crucified, risen Christ. It is Christ we must preach and live, Christ who is the center and circumference of our faith, Christ who is both our goal and the power to attain our goal. In one brilliant passage Paul describes this cosmic Christ:

> He is the image of the invisible God, the first-born of
> all creation; for in Him all things were created, in heaven
> and on earth, visible and invisible, whether thrones
> or dominions or principalities or authorities—all things
> were created through Him and for Him. He is before
> all things and in Him all things hold together
> (Colossians 1:15-17).

"And in Him all things hold together." It remains for us then to build bridges, linking an estranged, fallen world to its source and its salvation. If we cannot—will not—build the bridges, then what will become of the children?

Will Allen Dromgoole has captured the essence of our task in an old poem many will remember from school days. Its title? "The Bridge Builder."

> An old man going a lone highway
> Came in the evening cold and gray
> To a chasm vast and deep and wide.
> The old man crossed in the twilight dim,

The sullen stream had no fears for him,
But he stopped when safe on the other side
And built a bridge to span the tide.
"Old man," said a fellow pilgrim near,
"You are wasting your strength with building here;
Your journey will end with the ending day,
You never again will pass this way,
You've crossed the chasm deep and wide,
Why build you this bridge at evening tide?"
The builder lifted his old gray head,
"Good friend, in the path I have come," he said,
"There followeth after me today
A youth whose feet must pass this way.
This chasm which has been as naught to me
To that fair-haired youth might a pitfall be,
He, too, must cross in the twilight dim,
Good friend. I am building the bridge for him."

This world knows no shortage of builders. Walls and weapons and prejudices are in abundant supply. Many things—race, education, economics, politics—keep us isolated from one another . . . and from God. What is missing are those men and women of faith and vision who care enough to reach across the chasms which separate us, spanning the differences which keep us apart. But if only a few can be encouraged to volunteer, what a difference it will make for the children. And for us all.

6

The Good Samaritan

WILL ED WARREN

Jesus may well have been relating an actual occurrence in this well-known story. The road from Jerusalem to Jericho was known to be dangerous; its narrow passage and sharp curves were ideal for bands of robbers. In the early part of the 20th century, tourists were robbed along this road and the thieves escaped into the hills before police could be summoned. In fact, until recent times, travel along the Jericho road was hazardous without protection by a local strong man. Jesus' account of the mugging and robbing of the man in Luke's gospel is as contemporary as a modern newspaper report.

Lawyers of that day were experts in the law of Moses; the lawyer in this account wanted to test Jesus' grasp of the law. The question he posed to Jesus was, "Teacher, what shall I do to inherit eternal life?" Jesus replied, "What is written in the law? How do you read?" The lawyer replied as would any rabbi of that day, "You shall love the Lord your God with all your heart, and with all your soul, and with all your strength, and with all your mind; and your neighbor as yourself." Jesus told him, "You have answered right; do this, and you will live."

The lawyer then countered Jesus by asking, "And who is my neighbor?" To the Jews of that time a neighbor was a fellow Jew, and to the members of the Dead Sea community an accepted dictum was to love your neighbor and hate your enemy. The lawyer seized the moment to argue an old issue. He does not appear interested in the essence of religion nor in the core of faith but, instead, in a trivial pursuit of minutiae that only a legalist spirit could conceive. Too frequently Christians mirror this lawyer's attitude in their paralysis by analysis of current issues. Some of us prefer to talk or debate religion rather than be living examples of true religion. We debate the care of orphans but actually care for very few orphans. We debate how the gospel is to be preached but preach very little gospel. We debate the limits of fellowship but practice very little fellowship, even among ourselves. The potent power of Jesus' life was in His living example of true religion accompanied by His admonition that men follow His example (John 13:15).

The priest and Levite passed on either side of the injured and dying man on the Jericho road. In this situation, their religion had no relevance to daily life. The center of their religion was in the Temple, with no application to daily living. Their reactions were similar to the three ministers being interviewed individually by a television station. The interviewer gave careful attention to the responsibility of a Christian in a similar situation to that of the good Samaritan. Unknown to the ministers, a professional actor played the part of a derelict as he lay in an alley separating two television studios. Each minister was asked to go to the studio across the alley. As each walked across the alley, the actor cried for help. How many of the ministers do you imagine stopped to help? None. Not one offered to help the man who cried for help. They failed to apply their religion to a life event. It could be reasoned that their religion was confined primarily to a church building and to preaching sermons and teaching classes on the fine points of doctrine. Their preaching conceivably includes admonitions to practice Christianity in daily living, but admonition without example is pharisaical (Matthew 23:4).

A test of Bible knowledge was administered by a co-worker to a congregation to determine the content to be taught to various age levels. The first part of the test consisted of questions concerning factual knowledge of the Bible, and the second part was designed to determine whether a person could relate the message of the Bible to life situations. Participants did well on the first part of the test, but the second part was failed by most. This may be indicative that we are, as were the priest and Levite, unable to relate our religion to life. Conceptualization of abstract religion without application in concrete life experiences is a dangerous situation.

The priest and Levite surely had personal reasons for their failure to help the injured man. They may have reasoned that "I will become unclean if I touch him." Jewish priests could not expose themselves to situations that prevented their serving in the Temple. They may have reasoned that Temple service is more important than caring for one hapless victim of a robbery; after all, the Temple is God's house. Opposed to this attitude is Jesus' practice of touching the untouchables (Matthew 3:3) and associating with sinners (Luke 15:1, 2). Jesus loved the unlovable. For us to emulate Jesus, we must not fear contact with those in the squalor of life nor hesitate to take risks in service to others.

Another reason the priest and Levite may have offered for not helping the injured man is that "it would be too dangerous for me to help this man." The man may have been a decoy — left in the road to attract some unsuspecting sympathetic individual who would, in turn, be attacked and robbed. During a lecture I was giving in an inner-city church on the story of the good Samaritan, I emphasized that Christians must become involved in the lives of other people. The example was given of a local event in which a woman had been raped on the front porch of a nearby house. Although she screamed for help, no one came to her aid nor did anyone call the police from the privacy of his home. One by one the audience stood and said, "If we tried to help, the same could have happened to us!" and "They might burn our house down!" There appeared to be consensus that the best thing to do that night was to do nothing, and the only explanation for this harsh consensus is fear — a fear that outweighed human compassion.

We do indeed live in dangerous times. But has there ever been a time without danger? Paul suffered danger from numerous sources: rivers, false brethren, Gentiles, in the city, in the wilderness, and from all manner of other dangers (II Corinthians 11:26). Jesus came into this world to "seek and save the lost" (Luke 19:10, notwithstanding the attendant dangers. He risked His life and gave it freely for the benefit of others. And therein lies the essence of the cross! Our care for others has to be as all-encompassing as the love of Christ. How can we be willing to lay down our lives for others (I John 3:16) when we lack the common decency to come to the aid of a helpless victim?

"He does not deserve my help; it was his own fault; anyone who travels the Jericho road alone doesn't deserve my compassion," may have been another rationale of the priest and Levite for refusing to help the man. This poignant story teaches that we are to help anyone in need, and whether or not the person deserves our help is beside the point. Each of us desires the mercy of God rather than His justice; and none of us deserves His mercy. We are surrounded by many who are half dead: the drug addict, the alcoholic, the person with AIDS, the person grieving the loss of a loved one, and innumerable others. We have no choice but to do for them what God has done for us by showing them our mercy and our love. As the preacher for many years at the Strathmore Church of Christ in Detroit, Michigan, a congregation at the crossroads of a great city, I had frequent contact with people who came by the office seeking help. Some were deserving and some were not, and there was often no way to know the difference. The thought occurred often that God may not be as concerned with what the derelict does with any gift rendered as with what the Christian does in the situation. Jesus did not come into the world because we deserved His coming; He came because He loved us. How we choose to respond to His gift of love does not diminish the power of His gift. He died on the cross because of who He was, and how we decide to respond to His sacrificial death in no way diminishes the potency of His sacrifice. Are we not to follow His example? (I Peter 2:21).

The sensitivity of the Samaritan is remarkable. An impressive fact is that the Samaritan had only partial truth of the Scriptures; yet he evidences a deeper grasp of the meaning of religion than the teachers of the law from Jerusalem. Jesus may be more concerned with what you do than with how much you know. It is deeply disturbing to thinking Christians that some religious groups who possess only partial truth of the Scriptures exhibit more of the spirit of Christ than do some of us. Try to imagine whom Jesus would today describe as the good Samaritan. Some of my university students suggested that it might be a "punk rocker." Would that disturb you? The story of the good Samaritan disturbed the lawyer. The appeal to the reader here is to seriously consider the intent of Jesus' teaching about the good Samaritan.

The Samaritan was sensitive to human need. The man in the road was near death and may not have been capable of calling out for help; he may have been unaware that help was being rendered. Still the Samaritan helped him and, in so doing, he demonstrated that he saw with the eyes of Jesus and felt with the compassion of Jesus. Television has contributed to an insensitivity to human need on the part of many of us, and we tend to be passive when a fellow human is in trouble. It is even possible to sit in church beside a person whose heart is breaking and who finds it impossible to cry for help. The person may be an abused wife, an abused child, a divorced person, or one for whom life has lost all meaning. Unless we are sensitive, these "half dead" people may actually die.

A friend told the following story. On a Sunday evening, a visiting Christian couple responded to the invitation and asked for the prayers of the church to help them in their struggle. After services a few people greeted them, but no one expressed any real caring. That same night the couple committed suicide. In a moment of desperation they had turned to the church, only to discover a lack of sensitivity to their needs. It is not within the scope of this message to give concrete suggestions for specific responses to those who seek our help, but basic to any caring response is the absolute necessity for sensitivity to human need and the acceptance that anyone in need is our neighbor.

The Samaritan took care of the man in the road; he treated his wounds with oil and wine, bound them, and took him to an inn. The Samaritan was willing to become bloody and dirty in lifting the man onto his donkey and, of course, the donkey became bloody and dirty in the process. This story is dear to my heart because my Dad was crushed by a tractor that turned over on him. He lay in the bottom of a creek with the tractor on top of him for two hours before someone discovered him. When he was found, men were summoned from the nearby highway to lift the tractor off his body. Some unknown good Samaritan put my Dad's bloody, muddy, and dirty body in the back seat of his car and rushed him to the nearest hospital, where my Dad later died. I will always be grateful to that good Samaritan, whoever he is. To my Dad he showed the spirit of Christ in his compassion and his deed.

The Samaritan took the time to help. It is possible he lost an entire day. Consider the importance of this — helping others takes time. We cannot help people on an assembly-line basis. When we become involved in the lives of people, it will take our time and, without willingness to invest our time, we cannot be of help to others. Our time and what we do with it is what life is all about; when we give our time to help others, we are giving them of our life. Jesus was never too busy to help! No one was ever turned away by Jesus, and He never forgot His mission.

The Samaritan did what he could. He could not minister to the hurts of all mankind, but he could help this one lonely helpless man. We, like him, may not be able to help numerous people, but we can minister to the person with whom we work, to the people next door, to those in a nearby apartment, and even to the person sitting on the church pew next to us. These may be people others have left at our door (Luke 16:19-31); they may be those ravaged by the tragedy of life, as in our story. Whatever the situation, to emulate Jesus we will be moved with compassion and will minister to their needs.

This story began with the lawyer's question, "What shall I do to inherit eternal life?" Jesus' response was, "This do and you shall live." The lawyer questions, "Who is my neighbor?" and Jesus relates this story to illustrate to whom one may be a neighbor. Jesus then exhorts, "Go and do likewise." Jesus is the perfect neighbor. He spent His entire life helping others and that is, after all, the meaning of the cross. In a sense Jesus is the victim in this story; He was sick and hungry, thirsty and a stranger, and naked and in prison, and He said, "Truly, I say to you, as you did it to the least of these my brethren, you did it to me" (Matthew 25:31-46).

In another sense, Jesus is the good Samaritan in the story. He sees your needs; whoever you are and whatever your need, He is willing to help. The message of the cross calls through the centuries that Jesus loves you and He laid down His life in order to help you. He is willing to bring healing and forgiveness to you. He will even leave you with an open-ended charge account, "Whatever you ask in my name, I will do it . . . ." (John 14:13).

7

Reading the Signs

DAVID TARBET

For some of us, being able to read every billboard while negotiating through heavy freeway traffic is a way of enhancing self-image. It makes you feel good and establishes your identity. If you can read all the highway signs, it proves you're good at something — even if your wife and kids don't appreciate the significance of your accomplishment!

But life's greatest challenge is to read the "signs" of Jesus. (The noun and verb occurrences of the word translated "sign" appear 83 times in the New Testament.) Any word that occurs that often surely deserves a careful examination.

The signs of Jesus give insight into His compassion for the ill, neglected, and sorrowful. They show us His tender heart. But over and beyond His amazing tenderheartedness and compassion, there is a more fundamental purpose for His signs. Indeed, we could say the "bottom line" purpose for His supernatural acts was to establish His authority as the divine Son of God. Note these Bible verses:

". . . the works which the Father has granted me to accomplish, these very works which I am doing, bear me witness that the Father has sent me" (John 5:36).

". . . though you do not believe me, believe the works, that you may know and understand that the Father is in me and I am in the Father" (John 10:38).

"But these are written, that you may believe that Jesus is the Christ, the Son of God, and that believing you may have life in His name" (John 20:31).

"We Would See Jesus"

The Apostle Peter said Jesus was attested to be the Son of God by "mighty works and wonders and signs" (Acts 2:22). Each of these words is significant. Jesus' miracles were called "mighty works" because they were accomplished by the power of the Almighty God. They were "wonders" because they "amazed" the people who saw them. They were called "signs" because they pointed to something beyond themselves (as highway signs point toward a shopping mall or factory outlet). Of these three key terms, "sign" is the most important for purposes of this study. The ultimate purpose of Christ's miracles lies in the things to which the miracles pointed — the things they signified.

In commenting upon the "signs" of Jesus, R. H. Lightfoot has stated: "A sign performed by the Lord is a visible pointer to the invisible truth about Him who performs it." William Barclay put it like this: "A sign is an event or a deed which gives insight into the mind and heart of the person who performs it. It is a window into the personality of the person through whom it is done."

The healing of the paralytic is a clear example of how Jesus' miracles were both "mighty works, wonders, and signs" (Mark 2:1-12). The healing of this man was a "mighty work" because of the power of Almighty God that enabled him to rise, take up his pallet, and walk. It was a "wonder" because all who saw it were "amazed" saying, "We never saw anything like this!" It was a sign because it established the authority of Jesus to forgive sins. "But that you may know that the Son of Man has authority on earth to forgive sins," Jesus said to the paralytic, "I say to you rise, take up your pallet, and go home" (Mark 2:10-11).

Fundamental to understanding the miracles of Jesus is to see them as pointing to Jesus, God's Son and our only Savior. His signs "attested" Him (Acts 2:22), "glorified" Him (John 11:4), singled Him out, and lifted Him above all His contemporaries (John 3:2). They created faith in the hearts of sincere skeptics both among the curious (John 4:42) and among His doubting disciples (John 20:24-28). His signs proved that He had a unique relationship with the Father (John 10:38) and established His authority (Mark 2:10).

Jesus intended those who saw His miracles also see to the spiritual lessons to which the miracles pointed. Unfortunately, this did not always come to pass. Those who witnessed the feeding of the 5,000 were filled with amazement at the wonder of the miracle itself, but they did not see the deeper spiritual lessons to which that miracle pointed. Jesus said, "Truly, truly, I say to you, you seek me, not because you saw signs, but because you ate your fill of the loaves. Do not labor for the food which perishes, but for the food which endures to eternal life, which the Son of Man will give to you" (John 6:26-27). The multitudes sought Jesus because He worked miracles (in fact they wanted Him to perform more of them!), but they failed to see the miracles as "signs" pointing to deeper spiritual truths.

Through His wonders and signs we see Jesus in all His beauty. We understand Him better. We love Him more. Our faltering faith is strengthened. He draws us closer to His heart.

"Written for Our Instruction"

We have examined the purpose of Christ performing miracles, but what about the purpose for recording those miracles? The purpose for recording the wonderful works of Jesus Christ was not necessarily the same as the initial purpose for working the miracles. The record of His signs did indeed lead the reader to "believe that Jesus is the Christ" (John 20:31), but it did more than that. F. F. Bruce asserts: "As the gospel parables are oral lessons of the kingdom of God, so the gospel miracles are object lessons, acted parables of the kingdom."

It is important that we recognize that Matthew, Mark, Luke, and John were selective in the miracles which they recorded. They did not record all the mighty works which He performed. John said He did "many other signs" which were not recorded in the Scriptures (John 21:25). What motivated the writers to include some miracles and exclude others?

The basis of discrimination lay in the pressing issues confronting the growing church, and the applicability of each miracle to those issues. The miracles helped mature a young church in the faith. Just "beneath the surface," the miracles of Jesus had spiritual lessons which enables struggling churches and newborn believers to meet their daily challenges. A. B. Bruce suggested that "the miracles of Jesus might be viewed as parables . . . not . . . that they did not happen or that an original parable had been transformed into event through the wishful thinking of the early church," but as "intimations of redemption."

Craig L. Blomberg, writing in the *Journal of the Evangelical Theological Society* gives three key points of similarity between the miracles and parables of Jesus: 1) The miracles both reveal and conceal, acting as signs for believers while repelling unbelievers, just like the parables; 2) Even the disciples misunderstood the miracles, so as to provoke the identical type of reply from Jesus that He used when they misunderstood His parables; and 3) The synoptics consistently liken Jesus' miracles with His proclamation of the kingdom of God. Blomberg concludes: "Miracles, like parables, are therefore metaphors of the kingdom."

"And He Looked Intently"

Dynamic spiritual lessons are implied in each of the Lord's miraculous signs.

The miracle of the virgin birth (Matthew 1:23) is a marvelous witness to the power of the Almighty Creator, who infused life into the womb of Mary. But just "beneath the surface" of that wonderful event is a plethora of spiritual lessons. To the writer of Hebrews, the virgin birth signified that since Jesus partook of our "same nature," He is able to understand our frail human condition. He knows what it is to be afraid of death, to be tempted, and to suffer. He is able to deliver us from the fear of death, to be merciful and helpful in time of temptation (Hebrews 2:14-18). The miracle of the virgin birth points to a savior who understands our deepest human needs.

The miracle of turning water to wine (John 2:1-11) is also full of spiritual lessons. The believer recognizes it as a "sign" pointing to Jesus and to the Christian life as the unprecedented completeness of joy and fruitfulness. The empty lives have been "filled" — like six empty stone jars were filled to the brim. Our colorless existence has been changed to exciting, stimulating fullness — like water was changed to rich, red wine. Jesus offers the best life there is, none before or after has equaled the quality of the Christian life. And, it keeps getting better and better — as the best wine saved until the last! There is also the striking implication that Jewish rites and ceremonies have been fulfilled in Jesus; He has achieved what "Jewish rites of purification" could never achieve — total cleansing from sin. The Old Testament system has been replaced, and we are now under the law of Christ (I Corinthians 9:21).

The miracle of feeding the 5,000 (John 6:1-14) points to the bountiful blessings of a life centered on Jesus. It visualizes an eternal truth; those who "hunger and thirst for righteousness will be satisfied" (Matthew 5:6). We have come to "fulness of life" in Him (Colossians 2:10). He is the "Bread of Life" which sustains life. Those who are not His committed disciples remain undernourished, unsatisfied, unfulfilled. Early Christians went out with a message that all other leaders and religions had nothing in comparison to what Christ provides. The Christian life is not just a "better way" to live, it is the only way to live! Our bread enables us to survive death and endures to eternal life. What a nourishing!

The cursing of the fig tree (Mark 11:12-14, 20-24) is a visualized sermon. As the apostles stood gazing at the roots of the withered fig tree, Jesus said: "Have faith in God. Truly, I say to you, whoever says to this mountain, 'Be taken up and cast into the sea,' and does not doubt in his heart, but believes that what he says will come to pass, it will be done for him. Therefore I tell you, whatever you ask in prayer, believe that you will receive it, and you will" (Mark 11:23-24). To this very day, whenever the sign of the withered fig tree is reflected upon, Christians are challenged to pray in faith and are reminded of the marvelous potential of prayer to move mountains of hardship! The sign of the withered fig tree helps us appreciate verses like I Peter 3:12, 5:7, and James 1:6.

The miracles of the resurrection of Jesus (Matthew 28:6) packs a two-fold message which has not faded though almost 2,000 years have passed since the sign took place.

First, it says to those who refuse to repent of their sins, that there is doom to the sinner. It is "the sign of the prophet Jonah, that the men of Nineveh will arise at the judgment with this generation and condemn it; for they repented at the preaching of Jonah, and behold, something greater than Jonah is here" (Matthew 12:38-41).

Second, the resurrection speaks a message of personal hope to the Christian, for it is the assurance that he will rise with Christ at the last day. As the Scripture says: "If the Spirit of Him who raised Jesus from the dead dwells in you, He who raised Christ Jesus from the dead will give life to your mortal bodies also through His Spirit which dwells in you" (Romans 8:11). It is the assurance that just as we have "borne the image of the man of earth," we will certainly "bear the image of the Man of heaven" (I Corinthians 15:49). Our Jesus, who conquered death, "will change our lowly body to be like His glorious body" (Philippians 3:20-21). How confident the Christian can be in the victory of God! All of the suffering and heartache of this present world — including the persecution which confronted early saints on every hand — fades into insignificance in the light of the greatest sign of all.

Believers and unbelievers need to study the miracles of Jesus for their spiritual significance. For the most part, these reserves of divine truth are still untapped. Few believers are aware of the dynamic source of reassurance, joy, peace, and hope contained within the visualized object lessons of the kingdom which Jesus performed in the villages of Judea and Galilee. Teachers need to do more with the signs which the apostles carefully selected to meet the needs of God's people in every age, in every nation, at every level of spiritual maturity.

> I heard about His healing, of His cleansing pow'r revealing
> How He made the lame to walk again and caused the blind to see;
> And then I cried "Dear Jesus, come and heal my broken spirit,"
> I then obeyed His blest commands and gained the victory.

E.M. Bartlett

8

A Startling Announcement

TONY ASH

Jesus did say shocking things. One of the most shocking came as He and His disciples were admiring the temple. "As for these things which you see," He said, "the days will come when there shall not be left here one stone upon another that will not be thrown down." To get the impact of His words, try imagining how you would react if you heard the same things said about the national buildings in Washington, D.C.

This statement from the Lord is found in Luke 21:6, and that chapter of Luke is our text. It isn't on the list of the top ten favorite Scriptures for the average man. Most people know of these verses (called the apocalyptic discourse in the textbooks) for one of two reasons. They have been party to discussions in Bible classes which tried to decide where Jesus spoke of the destruction of Jerusalem, and where of His second coming. Or they have heard texts from this chapter used by preachers who have theories to advance about just when the Lord is going to return.

Our concern, however, will follow neither of these paths. However, we hope it will be truer to Jesus' intent in speaking the words.

It was the final week of the Lord's life. He and His disciples had spent their Jerusalem days in the temple and its vicinity. Their comment and His response led to the natural "when" and "what sign" from the disciples. In the ensuing speech Jesus warned them about false Christs (vss. 5f.). He spoke of wars and natural calamities to come (vss. 9-11). First, however, there would be persecutions visited upon His followers (vss. 12-19). Then He addressed the destruction of Jerusalem (vss. 20-24).

At this point His language undergoes a subtle change, and assumes a more symbolic nature, as he spoke of the coming of the Son of Man (vss. 25-28). Then, a parable of the fig tree, speaking of the coming kingdom and the immutability of God's word (vss. 30-33). Finally, Jesus warned the disciples against a carelessness that would leave them unprepared when He came again (vss. 34-36). These last words, sometimes given short shrift in discussions of the passage, I take to be the "bottom line" of what Jesus was saying.

In order to get into this passage, there are some things that we might notice. First, observe the sorts of events Jesus described. Some things happened because of the way the world and humans are, but there is no indication of direct divine causality (wars). Some things come because people are converted, so that they are the indirect results of God's action (persecutions). Some things are signs (recall the request in vs. 7). Two specific ones are given. One is in verse 20 — Jerusalem would be surrounded by armies. The second is in verses 25-27, in connection with the coming of the Son of Man. Finally, some things are non-signs. There would be wars and calamities. People might consider them signs of the end, but Jesus said "the end will not be at once" (vs. 9). Perhaps Jesus said these things because some people expected non-signs to be signs, and then they concluded when He did not return after the non-signs that Jesus would not come again at all.

Another way into this material is to observe the dangers Jesus said His people would face. This approach shows how personally involved Jesus' hearers would be in what He said. They were in danger of being deceived by false Christs (vs. 8). They were in danger of being frightened by news of wars and revolutions (vs. 9). They were in danger of persecution for Christ's sake and the accompanying anxiety about how to make a defense. This persecution would rupture the closest of human ties, and would cause them to be hated by all men — and who wants to be hated by anyone (vss. 12-19)? There was danger in the destruction of Jerusalem. They might be caught in the city. More, they could be demoralized by the end of the established order. They might wonder, since Christianity came out of Israel, if, with the end of Jerusalem,

Christianity would survive. Finally, they were in danger of having their hearts weighed down by dissipation, drunkenness, and cares of this life, and thus being unready for Jesus' return (vss. 34-36).

How were the disciples to respond to these circumstances? Jesus told them not to follow false Christs. They were not to be terrified by wars — wars did not signal the end. In persecution they were to bear witness to their faith with God-given words. By standing firm they would save themselves. When Jerusalem was surrounded by armies, they were to get away or stay away from the city. When the Son of Man returned, they were to stand and lift their heads, for their redemption was near. At all times they were to be careful, watching and praying so they could stand before the Son of Man.

A final (fourth, if you have counted) way into the text is to notice what God would do. In persecution He would give them words to say. The text implies the destruction of Jerusalem was His act of punishment. He would give signs, and the Son of Man would come in power and great glory. God's word must come to pass. It is more sure than the heavens and the earth. All men would be aware of the second coming, and all would be called to appear before the Son of Man.

In a moment we want to consider why Jesus gave this speech at all. Before that, let us make three observations. First, Jesus indicated that history will take place between His two comings. This was what the angels implied in Acts 1:9-11. All life, therefore, is to take its character for the fact that Jesus will come again, and men will be held accountable. Every deed, word, thought takes its significance from the realization that events move toward God's conclusion. The second observation is that God controls history. It is not haphazard or meaningless but moves toward His goal. Finally, this second coming will come at an unexpected time. That is, there will be no announcement beforehand telling when it will occur, and consequently the only way to be ready at any time is to be ready all the time.

Why did Jesus make this speech? It was not to give some time-setting scheme by which people could interpret history in advance and foretell the date of the second coming. All such speculations obscure Jesus' real intent. His real purpose came from the love He had for His followers. He came to earth for them. He spent much time training and nurturing them. He wanted them (as He wants all) to become what God intended them to be. But He was aware of dangers and wanted to avert the tragedy of their falling away. So He warned them, in order that when they no longer could experience Him in person, their trust in the invisible God would be unwavering. Ultimately, He wanted them to share in the triumph for which God had designed them. That is why verse 28, about the victory at the second coming, is so important. If they were redeemed, nothing else mattered. If they were not, their lives were failures. Jesus did not want them to make something which was less important than redemption more important than redemption.

When Luke wrote these words, after his research (Luke 1:1-4), it was several decades later. Though the date is still disputed, we are going to assume it was after 70 A.D., and that Jerusalem had been destroyed by the Romans. Because some of the same observations are pertinent to us, let us briefly notice how Luke's readers would read these words. They would know that many of the events Jesus foretold had taken place. Jesus had predicted the future. Thus God does control history, and one can confidently assume that He will act in the future and that Jesus will come again. For them (and us) there was only one sign left to look for.

Several decades had passed, and despite the intense expectations of the early Christians, Jesus had not returned. They would probably have concluded "we are in this for the long haul, we may die before He comes." That would give life a different perspective. The key would be constant readiness.

Because they would know some who had left the faith, the warnings of Jesus could have special impact. And finally, the church did continue, and thrived, despite the end of Jerusalem.

Now, these many centuries later, what can we find here that speaks to our lives? We can be reminded by Jesus' words that we, too, live between His two comings. We should examine our value systems and priorities in life to see if they reflect that view of things. Do we tend to ascribe ultimate priority to the here and now? Do we buy into the limited goals of our culture? Have we put our ultimate trust in things that are not ultimate? Though we may intellectually affirm that He will come again, it is always appropriate to examine our lifestyles to see if they are consistent with our affirmations.

Luke 21 also reminds us how much Jesus cares about His people. Again and again in the biblical story He showed concern for their spiritual welfare. Even in Gethsemane, as Luke tells it, both before and after His own agonized prayer, Jesus encouraged His disciples to watch and pray lest they enter into temptation. Jesus knew the tragedy if He were to return and find none ready. In a sense, His whole work would be undone.

The chapter indicates disciples could be led from their faith by wars, natural calamities, suffering, and the passing of the established order. Aside from the obvious consequences, such events could create enough anxiety that concerns for God could be driven out. Or they could lead people to believe that God does not control the world, for, if He did, He would not let such things happen. Jesus knew that such things could create a change of perspectives, leading to dissipation (life lived with no moral restraints whatever), drunkenness, and extreme anxiety. Anxiety, the opposite of trust, tempts man to rely only on self. Seeing the inadequacy of that ground of confidence, man is driven to despair about life.

So Jesus warned about what might happen. God is more concerned that we be saved than we are to be saved. He is more concerned we be faithful than we are concerned to be faithful. Even when we despair and give up on ourselves, He does not give up. God never deserts man, and Jesus wants His disciples encouraged by that knowledge.

We learn also that if God cares so much for our survival, we ought to be deeply concerned about our Christian brothers and sisters who have lapsed in their faith. How can we reach them and thus demonstrate Jesus' care for them? Some studies have shown that one of the greatest causes of departure from the Christian community is lack of significant friendships within the body. If this is true, then we do well to develop those friendship skills by which we can win back those who have left, and so draw them into the love of a rich fellowship that they too can know the victory.

Jesus reminds us that He will return unexpectedly. He had given such warnings before, in Luke 12:35-48 and 17:22-37. It might seem convenient to know just exactly when Jesus will return. Then at the last minute we could shine our lives up and present them to God for the reward. But God doesn't want this. He wants people who live for Him. He wants a certain type of person, not last-minute bargainers. Probably one reason God has not told us when is because the clue is to always be ready. This, after all, is the way real Christian joy is found. One suspects people who want a last-minute warning in order to prepare haven't gotten the message about what Christianity really is.

Finally, there is the victory. It isn't easy to be a faithful Christian for an entire lifetime. Many do not make it. Those who do survive through difficulties. There are numerous occasions when we want to give up. But we persevere, sometimes only just barely, and finally know the indescribable and unimaginable triumph implied in the words of verse 28. "Look up and raise your heads, because your redemption is drawing near."

9

I Have Called You Friends

HARVEY PORTER

I like this time of the year. People sometimes have open houses and invite friends and loved ones in. We send cards to each other and thank each other for our friendship and our love, especially in the Lord. I was thinking about what a cherished relationship friendship is, and I remembered that in the Old Testament only one person was called "the friend of God." It was Abraham. Not only do the Jews call Abraham the father of their nation, but so do those of the Arab world, for they, too, are his descendants through Ishmael, who was the son of Abraham by the slave woman, Hagar. Some of their houses of Islam worship, which are called mosques, bear names, and most common is the name that is *Ibrahim el Khalil*. It literally means "Abraham, the friend of God."

It is an overwhelming thought to realize that the God of the universe condescends to be in an intimate relationship with a mortal. Yet the Scriptures say that Abraham was one of the three men who walked with God. We know that he was known for his faith. The supreme test of his faith was when God asked him to sacrifice his only son, Isaac. Abraham was a friend of God because he chose to be, and nothing in this world could deter their friendship. There are three places in the Bible where Abraham is called a friend of God. In II Chronicles 20:7

God says, "I know Jacob who is the offspring of Abraham, my friend." Abraham is called a friend of God in Isaiah 41:8 and in James 2:23. James says "Abraham believed God, and it was credited to him as righteousness, and he was called the friend of God." Likewise, our faith identifies us with Abraham, and we too become friends of God. I am simply saying that if we believe in God and believe in our Lord Jesus Christ, then our belief is going to bring about a friendship.

Now I want to ask you a question. Do you know how many people our Lord called "friend"? He used this word on three different occasions, and I would like for us to look at those three and make a personal application to our own lives to see if we really are friends of the Lord Jesus Christ.

In John 11:11 He called Lazarus "friend" and in John 15:14 He said to His apostles, "you are my friends . . ." Then, to our astonishment, He called Judas Iscariot "friend."

It seems that we are in an age where perhaps we are too busy to develop the kind of friendships that used to exist when the pace of life was slower. I can remember my dad going at any hour of the night to sit with a sick friend. I can remember hearing him speak of a man whom he loved. He said, "He is my best friend." They were very close, and if either one needed the other, he would be there.

Our mobile society has made it more difficult to form long, lasting friendships. But we are made richer by genuine friendships that we have made the effort to nurture. Friendship is one of those sacred relationships in life that is very close to the nature of God Himself.

If we think of friendship as something that is secondary to love, then we do not have the true idea of what biblical friendship is. This is not a casual friendship, such as when we say of an acquaintance, "I have known him for a long time; we are friends." Would we go out of our way for him? Would we sacrifice for him? Are we easily offended when he does not do just what we think he ought to do? And when we are disappointed, do we say, "This is the end of our friendship"? Or would we fight for a friendship? Do we seek to maintain it? Will we let nothing come between us? I am talking about the kind of friendship that you and I enjoy as fellow members of God's family. Not only are we brethren, but we are friends in the Lord Jesus Christ. We are friends with Him and consequently friends with one another. This is a biblical concept. Maybe we have not thought of friendship in that light.

Now let us look at the three instances in which Jesus used the word "friend." In Matthew 26:49ff., Matthew records this incident. It was the night of our Lord's betrayal. He was in the Garden of Gethsemane. Judas came to Jesus and said, "Hail, Master," and kissed Him. Jesus' answer is rather enigmatic and is translated in various ways, but the New International Version reads, "Friend, do what you came for." Jesus called him friend!

The Greek word that is translated here as "friend" is *hetairos*. Judas was the only person whom Jesus addressed by this term. It expresses a concept of friendship that we often use, such as when we call someone a friend and then say, "Well, we are not close friends; we are casual acquaintances. We ride to work together, but we are not on intimate terms." By calling Judas "friend," Jesus was using this term that Judas would have understood: comrade, companion. It is sometimes described as a kindly address in which we would speak to someone, and by calling him "friend," would be showing our willingness to be friends. I believe this is exactly what our Lord was seeking to do.

Did Judas want to be close to the Lord? He could have. Our Lord is open to anyone who seeks Him. There are people you cannot make friends with. There are people you will never get close to. It is not their nature and they do not want it. But this is not true with Jesus. It was no fault of His that He could not call Judas by the intimate word for friend. Judas was one who never entered the inner circle. He was that one whose love had been diluted by personal ambition and materialism. Why did he betray the Lord? I do not believe for a moment that he had animosity toward Jesus or thought Jesus was going to be put to death. I believe he loved the Lord, but it was not a strong love. The evidence seems to say that he wanted to force Jesus into the role of an earthly king, to drive out the Romans, and to set up His kingdom, making the apostles ambassadors or men of state. He had seen the power of Jesus in the miracles He had performed and he knew there was nothing the Lord could not do. When Jesus saw him in the garden, He did not call him a traitor. Our Lord chose the lesser word for friendship, which may indicate that Jesus was still desirous of true friendship with Judas. Although Judas had been offered the opportunity for intimate friendship, he never availed himself of it. For Jesus said of him, "He who shares my bread has lifted up his heel against me."

Friendship? Judas did not seek it. Jesus did seek it. Did He keep the door open? Oh, yes, even to the last He still said, "Friend, what you do, do quickly."

Jesus called Lazarus "friend" (John 11:11). Here He used the Greek word *philos*, which is usually translated by the word "love." *Philos* has made its way into our language. "Philadelphia" means "brotherly love." It is not the word *agape*, which is the kind of love that God has, even for His enemies or people who do not love Him. It is part of God's great nature and His design for the salvation of the human family to love sinners, the unlovable.

Philos, however, is the love that is between two who desire each other's company. *Philos* expresses itself in affection and terms of endearment. It is the kind of love that occurs in a happy marriage relationship. We cannot use this word in the biblical sense without saying, "I love my friend." This is what Jesus called Lazarus: *philos*, friend.

Remember the touching story of the resurrection of Lazarus in John 11? Our Lord was with the apostles across the river Jordan, over on the eastern side in the land of Perea. Word was sent to Him that Lazarus was at the point of death. Jesus purposely delayed His journey until Lazarus had died. Then He said, "Our friend Lazarus has fallen asleep, but I go to wake him out of sleep. The apostles said to Him, 'Lord, if he has fallen asleep he will recover.' Now Jesus had spoken of his death, but they thought he meant taking rest in sleep. Then Jesus told them plainly, 'Lazarus is dead. And for your sake I am glad that I was not there so that you may believe. Let us go to him.' " It is apparent that the disciples knew that the Jews had been trying to capture Jesus and put Him to death, and they realized that his could be their last journey with Jesus. They wanted to be with Him even to the end.

Do not call Thomas "doubting Thomas." The Scriptures never do. Some clever preacher tacked that name on to Thomas and we have repeated it. Thomas did doubt at one time, but our Lord forgave him, so let us forgive him too and rather remember him for his courage. He said, "Let us go with Him that we may die with Him." Jesus and the apostles returned to Bethany, where Jesus had spent many happy hours in the home of Mary and Martha and Lazarus. When Jesus arrived at the tomb, He wept. And the next verse says, "And they that beheld Him said, 'See how He loved him.' "

He did love him. He called him friend. He said, "Our friend Lazarus has died." Our Lord was touched, not only by his death but by the sorrow of Mary and Martha.

Can you see the contrast between the two words for "friend" that Jesus used in referring to Judas and to Lazarus? One was a distant friend;

the other, a close friend. An expression of love. How tender and how beautiful. The latter is the kind of relationship that you and I are seeking with our Lord Jesus Christ. He not only is our savior, our king, and our elder brother, but He is our friend. We love to sing that great old song, "What A Friend We Have in Jesus."

Gerhard Kittel, in his monumental work on the Greek words of the New Testament, described the earliest meaning of the word *philos* as "that which is intrinsic, that which belongs to." What does it mean, "to be intrinsic"? Intrinsic means "on the inside." It is what two hearts possess in common, their love, their experiences, their secrets, their goals. They are drawn together by sharing the same love for Jesus, His word, and the church.

Consider Lazarus. He loved God, and when Jesus said, "I am His Son," he loved Jesus. And when Jesus said, "This is God's will," he did it because he loved Jesus. They shared all of these things. He wanted to be with Jesus. They were intrinsic. They were intimate. They were close. They were inside each other. Friends who have loved each other for years begin to think like each other, and, as in a good marriage, the two truly become one flesh. Love has that binding power. Love has that holding power. Is not it interesting that the word for friend is the word for love; they are used interchangeably. Our Lord said about Lazarus, "Our friend, the one whom we love, Lazarus, has died." The other idea that is found in the original meaning of *philos* is, "belonging to." "Our friend, Lazarus. He belongs to us and we belong to him." This should not seem strange to us. Has not our Lord bought us? Are not we the sheep of His pasture? Are not we His brethren? Are not we His family? Are not we His church? Are not we His bride? Do not we belong to Him? Our preaching has not emphasized the fact that we are friends with our Lord, but we are. We have the same values, the same love, and Lazarus shared all of these. He belonged to Jesus. How beautiful!

The third time Jesus used the word friend is in John 15:14: "You are my friends if you do what I have commanded." Historically our emphasis on this passage has been on our submission to the Lord, rather than on our friendship with Him. Our friendship truly motivates us to obey Him. As His friend it would be unthinkable that we would do anything to disappoint or hurt Him.

When our Lord said, "You are my friends," He was speaking to the apostles, who were His immediate hearers, but secondarily to us, who hear through His word. What He said to them, He is saying to all of us. We too have the right and the privilege of being friends with the Lord of lords and the King of kings, the divine Son of God. It is a thought too great to comprehend. In the context of this passage Jesus said, "I have called you bondservants, slaves, but now I call you friends." It is as though He is saying, "I am taking you into the close relationship with me." He said, "No master reveals unto his slave the things of his heart, but I am calling you no longer slaves." And yet are not we His slaves? He paid the price for us. By His blood we have been cleansed. We are His kingdom and we are here to serve. We must never forget that. But here is the joy of our situation: His feeling toward us is that, even as we serve, we are not slaves, we are friends. And what do friends do? They serve one another. The motivation for their service is not fear or a sense of obligation; it is love. That is what friends are. Here is the role of all mankind before God. Not only do we want to serve God, but by His grace He has elevated us to this noble position, that of friends. As friends we have the privilege of intimacy with Him. That closeness does not depend upon our Lord; it depends upon you and me. This determines how close we draw, how much we pray, how much we give, how much we think of Him, how much we enjoy fellowship with one another because of our common Lord. There is no religion in the world like this! No other religious leader has ever said as Jesus said, "You are my friends if you do whatever I command you."

I hope you have obeyed Him and thereby become His friend by joining Him in a death, burial, and resurrection to walk in newness of life with Him. He is your constant companion. He is your bosom friend. There are things in your life that no one will know but you and Jesus and God. He will share and bless and love, and He will enrich you as His friend for life.

10

Bruised for Our Iniquities

CHARLES HODGE

> He was despised and rejected by men; a man of sorrows, and acquainted with grief; and as one from whom men hide their faces he was despised, and we esteemed him not. Surely he has borne our griefs and carried our sorrows; yet we esteemed him stricken, smitten by God, and afflicted. But he was wounded for our transgressions, he was bruised for our iniquities; upon him was the chastisement that made us whole, and with his stripes we are healed.
>
> Isaiah 53:3-5

It was my privilege to sit in Dr. Pack's first classes at Abilene Christian University. He gave depth, scholarship, and freshness to our learning. I was also selected to mimic him on "All Students Day" there in 1952. It was fun to "walk like" and "gesture" as he; it is now a humbling privilege to follow in his steps. This is my wholehearted thanks!

Introduction

Isaiah 53 is "Holy Ground" in Scripture. Things revealed there are so poignant we are afraid to touch them. Great songs and sermons have come from this fountain. Yet neglected is a study of "bruised." The Lamb was bruised!

Pull out your concordance. Satan's head was bruised in Genesis 3:15; Jesus at Nazareth in Luke 4:18 promised to set at liberty them that are bruised. To be bruised is to be spoiled, ruined, crushed. There can be no stronger expression in Hebrew. Jesus, in total darkness, died without any resources. He was made to be sin who had no sin. The "Man Forsaken" was also the "God Forsaken."

Justice

God is not a "Walking Civil War." His attributes do not ebb and flow; they do not battle. God is God is God. There never was more injustice than at the cross. It was the just for the unjust. This is the heart of the heart of the heart. Jesus not only had physical pain but "our feelings" (Hebrews 4:15). He was denied, betrayed, rejected, blasphemed, left alone, without resource. Man in sin could not save himself. Jesus paid what we could not pay. He bought what we could not buy!

God suffered! This is mind-boggling! It is hard for humans to conceive. Read Hebrews 5:7. Jesus had cryings and prayers. Mercy did not cheat justice. Jesus was in an agony unto death (Matthew 26:38). The law demanded death. God provided the Lamb (John 1:29, 36). Jesus was numbered with the transgressors; however, He was not a transgressor. The cross is not sentimentalized garbage — it is costly grace. The cross is the answer of an outraged God of justice to a bunch of hell-bound sinners. Read 2 Corinthians 5:19-21; Ephesians 2:14-16; Hebrews 2:10; 1 Peter 1:18, 19; 2:24. But not only is the cross the revealing of God's grace — it is equally a revealing of man's revolting sin! Therefore the many statements about atonement — vicarious, sacrifice, ransom, expiation, propitiation, imputation, substitutionary.

The Sovereignty of God

In the first gospel sermon (Acts 2:23-36), Peter placed the cross under the sovereignty of God. The cross was heaven-directed. God suffered as man, for man, and with man. God poured out heaven's wrath upon Jesus. Myths die hard! Man still thinks God changes. He was wrath in the Old Testament and love in the New Testament. He was merciful at the cross; He will pour out wrath at the judgment. Either Jesus died for my sin or I will die for my sin! Heaven and hell stand together! Grace demands hell. If there is no hell there should be! To deny hell is to reject grace.

Read Revelation 6:16, "The wrath of the Lamb." We can grasp wrath from the "Lion," but not from a "Lamb"! God sent Jesus from glory to the grave that we might go from the grave to glory! Jesus met the stipulations, bore the curses, and earned the blessings! WHAT A GOD! WHAT A SAVIOR! WHAT A SALVATION!

Can man in sin be saved? If so, how, when, where, and by whom? God cannot save a sinner without satisfying justice. The cross did not change God's mind about sin — it demonstrated it. God is a friend! God is "my" friend. The sin problem was cured at the cross! If not at the cross then where?

"IT PLEASED GOD" "I wanted to do it." God is not morbid — He had no personal pleasure in the cross. But since it had to be done, He wanted to do it! John 3:16 is the Golden Text of the Bible. God's love is the only permanent motivation in Christianity (2 Corinthians 5:14; 1 Corinthians 15:10). We love because God first loved us (1 John 4:7-11). Salvation is not merely a business transaction. It is not that God paid 50 cents and man pays 50 cents. JESUS PAID IT ALL! There is nothing justice demands, sin requires, or man needs that Jesus has not provided!

Jesus simply said, "It is finished." He said that because man can never fathom the depths of "Amazing Grace." There is no other way! If God could have saved man any other way, then He is a friend and not God! God did not send Christ to die to prove love. This is absurd! Killing sons does not prove love; it only proves insanity! But sin demands death (Genesis 2, Romans 6:23). God offered His Son in our stead! This is incomprehensible love (2 Corinthians 9:15). GOD WANTED TO! While I was a student at Abilene Christian University, my Mama had surgery requiring a blood transfusion. I gave that blood! I wanted to! God was not reluctant! His full heart was in it! The question is not, "Would a good God send a man to hell?" but, "Can a just God save hell-bound sinners?" God cannot violate Himself. But He did provide.

God did not stand by in vengeful anger demanding full restitution for a broken law or offended honor . . . but the exact opposite. In infinite love, compassion, and mercy God involved Himself in our plight while we were helpless and damned in our sins (Romans 5:6-8). In Jesus, God took the penalty of sins upon Himself, gathering all our evil into His pure heart. This was not mechanical substitution but profoundly personal love. God is BOTH the just and the justifier. AMAZING GRACE! This is the gospel of the grace of God:

Love so amazing, so divine
Demands my life, my soul, my all.

Grace and the Gospel

The Great Commission is to preach the gospel (Mark 16:15, 16). The gospel is what God did for man; the gospel is "Good News." Tell men what God did before you tell men what to do. Do not turn the "Good News" into "Bad News." This simply means that Christianity is "person-centered" not "issue-centered." Christianity is Christ. Center upon Christ. Convert sinners to Christ; keep saints in Christ. The issue is not my love for God but His love for me! The more I grasp this love, the more I respond.

The gospel is not our obligation to perform in order to receive a gift. The truth — because of the gift I am obligated. One does not repent in order to earn grace; because of grace one repents! Man is prone to forget what God did for him. We preach human activity rather than heavenly grace. The Lord's Supper, weekly, should remind us that we were bought with a price. "And I, if I be lifted up from the earth, will draw all men unto me. This He said, signifying what death He should die" (John 12:32, 33). Read also John 3:14-16.

Grace is channeled through faith (Romans 1:14-17). It is "faith from beginning to end." It is all of grace. Jesus paid it all. Man has no merit. Man trusts, accepts, claims, appropriates what God did in Christ on the cross. This faith is in Christ, not faith per se. Sectarians "believe in believing." Their faith is in their faith. This reduces, paradoxically, faith into a work. Faith is total dependence, surrender, and commitment to Christ. His righteousness is our hope; His name is our power of attorney.

Baptism, actually, is what God does! Man hears, believes, repents, confesses — but is baptized by another! Baptism is a visible, physical, historical demonstration of total faith in another — Jesus Christ. In baptism God adopts us into His body, the church. Baptism is not human merit; it is the very opposite. Baptism is man's confession of human inadequacy and total commitment to Jesus.

GRACE! What man needs yet resists! We live in a "God helps those who help themselves" world. Christianity can become human sufficiency.

Man wishes to be "self-made." Grace is a gift; Christ is that gift. A gift can be accepted; it cannot be earned. A gift cannot be repaid. Grace is threatening to human autonomy. It is hard for human pride to admit we are at the mercy of love. It is devastating for sinners to profoundly admit, finally, that they are saved by grace. Christians are accepted in the Beloved (Ephesians 1:16). "Accept your acceptance."

Conclusion

Read Philippians 2:5-11. Familiar Scripture needs to be read more closely. Most read/hear the word, "shall." The word is not "shall'; it is "should." Since we have heard the word as "shall," the judgment has been inserted into Philippians 2. We have in mind a unison confession at the judgment. This may be true. God can do as He wills. However, this is unlike God! God does not coerce, pressure, abuse the free moral agency of man. Christianity is volunteer.

SHOULD! What a thought! Since Jesus died for us — at His name — our knees should bow and our tongues should confess! This is the only response! This is the attitude/mentality of believers! This is not done once — twice. This is the Christian lifestyle. Jesus is the Lord of my life because He died for my sins!

Preach Jesus Christ and Him crucified!

11

The Imprint of the Nails

MIKE ARMOUR

Had I been there two thousand years ago, among the sun-baked hills of Galilee, would I have believed He was the Son of God? He was obviously a man of exceptional gifts — perhaps even the Messiah.

But the Son of God? That's an altogether different matter. When you stand close enough to smell the sweat on a man's body, it is difficult to believe that he is divine.

Yet, there were those who believed. Their numbers were never great, to be sure. But they were believers, nonetheless. They experienced Him in the fullness of His humanity, only to confront the certainty that He was somehow more than human.

How many nights they saw Him by the fire, exhausted from the push and press of an ever-present crowd. But even when they saw Him drawn and wearied they could not miss something extraordinary about Him. When He spoke, the words seemed to emanate from the very throne room of heaven. And when they looked into His eyes they caught the reflection of majesties past and the anticipation of glories to come.

Thus, while others might think of Him as John the Baptist or Elijah or one of the other prophets resurrected, for them only one conclusion was appropriate: "Thou are the Christ, the Son of the living God."

While they were still struggling with that concept, however, He began to speak of an imminent betrayal. To them such talk seemed nonsense. How could the Son of God possibly die? Yet, when they objected He quickly silenced them. Their very words, He warned, placed them in league with the evil one.

And then, in the week of His greatest success, with the echoes of His triumphal entry still reverberating through the alleyways of Jerusalem, the very calamity He had foretold came to pass. By the agency of a betrayal kiss and at the insistence of a maddened mob, He was led in seeming helplessness to Golgotha.

The disciples fled in confusion, unable to explain this sudden turn of events. Had their trust in Him been misplaced? Had their hopes no foundation?

Thus, before returning to the Father, Jesus had to teach one final lesson. At His feet the disciples had already learned two difficult and demanding truths: first, that Jesus of Nazareth was the Son of God, and second, that the Son of God was to die. Now He must teach them that the Son of Man would rise again.

John 20 commends itself to us as the most thorough account of how Jesus undertook that task. That chapter finds Jesus contending with entrenched skepticism, not among His gainsayers, but within His own inner circle of close friends. The chapter gives us an opportunity to observe how He dealt with at least four different kinds of skepticism which stood between the disciples and their faith in the resurrection.

First was emotional skepticism, seen in the person of Mary of Magdala. Here was a woman so controlled by emotion that she seemed incapable of clear thought. Even when the truth presented itself compellingly, she failed to grasp it.

John says that she came to the tomb "early on the first day of the week, while it was still dark." She then ran to the disciples to say, "They have taken the Lord out of the tomb, and we don't know where they have put him" (John 20:1-2).

But that simply was not true. Luke, providing details omitted in John's account, relates a conversation several women (including Mary) had held with angels at the tomb. The angels told them, "He is not here; He has risen! Remember how He told you while He was still with you in Galilee: 'The Son of Man must be delivered into the hands of sinful men, be crucified and on the third day be raised again.' " Luke then notes that the women "remembered His words" (Luke 24:1-8).

Mary's report to the disciples, however, said nothing of a resurrection. Instead, she suggested that the body had been stolen. Nor was she easily shaken from her persuasion. Later, on returning to the tomb, she told the supposed gardener, "They have taken my Lord away and I don't know where they have put Him" (John 20:10-14).

Nothing illustrates Mary's blind emotionalism more clearly than the casual way in which she conversed with angelic beings. Most of us would be caught up short by even a single encounter with angels. But on this particular morning Mary conversed with angels not once, but twice. Yet she acted as though nothing out of the ordinary had occurred.

In verse 13 and again in verse 15 the question is put to her, "Why are you crying?" Had she only listened to what was being said, had she only opened her eyes to what she was witnessing, she would have realized that there was no reason to weep. But she had allowed her emotions such license that she was oblivious even to persistent truth.

Unfortunately, Mary was hardly the last person to struggle with emotional skepticism. Anger over the death of a loved one or outrage at some unrepaired injustice keeps thousands from believing in God. For others faith is impeded by deep attachments to their family or loyalty to a religious heritage. Like Mary, such people hear without hearing. They see without seeing. Emotions have blinded them to the truth.

We see another kind of skepticism when we look at Peter's actions in John 20. For lack of a better term, we will refer to his doubts as dispositional skepticism. Following Mary's report of the empty tomb, Peter and John ran to see for themselves. Peter arrived first and examined the linen strips which had once wrapped the body of Jesus. Then John came on the scene. Verse eight says that he "saw and believed."

John graciously does not mention the reaction of Peter. Luke tells us, however, that Peter "went away, wondering to himself what had happened" (Luke 24:12). Luke's verb *thaumazo*, "to wonder", connotes one who stares at a thing, unable to explain it. Thus, in contrast to John, who went away believing, Peter went away bewildered.

The simultaneous appearance of these two disciples at the tomb affords an invaluable insight into how that faith is formed. Here are two men, reared in the same villages, apprenticed in the same vocation, trained in the same synagogues, called by the Lord at the same time and together with Him at all the major events of His ministry — these two men, so very much alike in their background, came to the same place at the same time on the same morning and both saw the same thing. Yet one went away believing, while the other went away bewildered.

Their reactions are instructive. They tell us that compelling evidence alone will not bring about faith. Evidence which was persuasive to John served only to confuse Peter. How could one of these men believe, while the others did not? The answer must be found in the disposition of their hearts.

Not uncommonly we walk away from unsuccessful evangelistic endeavors blaming ourselves for the failure. We tell ourselves that we could have won this person for the Lord had we only known how to present the case for Christ more cogently. But while evangelistic methods are important, and while we should never tire of perfecting our witness, we must never forget that conversion requires something more than method and persuasion. As with Peter and John, compelling evidence only yields faith when the disposition of the heart is proper.

As we move from Peter to the rest of the disciples, John 20 reveals still another type of skepticism. We shall call this form practical skepticism, doubt which manifests itself in the way we go about daily life. We see evidence of such skepticism when the disciples come together on the evening of that resurrection Sunday. John 20:19 describes them as meeting with "the doors locked for fear of the Jews."

Somehow these friends of Jesus had not grasped the implication of the resurrection. No excuse remained for them to continue to believe Him dead. The women had reported their conversations with the angels. John had returned to tell what he had seen. Mary had even talked with Him personally in the garden. And by now the two disciples from Emmaus had hurried back to Jerusalem to report their lengthy discourse with Him (Luke 24:13-36).

If these reports were true — and they all seemed to corroborate one another — why was there reason to fear? If this man Jesus, who loved them, had triumphed over death, why tremble at the petty power of their enemies?

Yet there they were, huddled in fear behind closed doors. Little wonder that the Lord's first words to them were, "Peace be with you" (John 20:19-21), or that He repeated that blessing two verses later. Until they shook off this paralyzing fear, they could never be effective witnesses of His resurrection.

But practical skepticism exerts a tenacious hold. A week later Jesus came to the disciples a second time, only to find them still behind locked doors (John 20:26). By now there should have been no question in their minds that He was alive. After all, they had seen and talked to Him themselves. But they had not "internalized" the truth of the resurrection so that it reshaped their behavior. Thus, Jesus greeted them once more with the words, "Peace be with you."

Jesus also used this second visit to contend with a fourth form of skepticism in John 20, the forthright disbelief of Thomas. Absent when Jesus made His first appearance to the disciples, Thomas would not be persuaded by their testimony. To him only one proof would suffice: "Unless I see the nail marks in His hands and put my finger where the nails were, and put my hand into His side, I will not believe it" (John 20:24-25).

This attitude constitutes what we might call empirical skepticism. Empiricism is the pursuit of truth that can be ascertained through the five senses. Radical empiricism (such as philosophical positivism) says, "Unless I can measure it or quantify it or analyze it in a laboratory, I will not believe it." Because God can be subjected to none of these tests, the strict empiricist insists that no proof of God's existence is possible. The empiricist denies the resurrection for the same reason.

But numerous realities, all universally acknowledged, resist empirical proof. The subconscious is one such reality. No one seriously doubts its existence. But how do we prove that existence? We cannot quantify the subconscious. We cannot measure it. Laboratories can only examine its effects (dreams, hypnotic experiences, etc.), not the subconscious itself.

In short, empiricism alone is an inadequate litmus of truth. We can "prove" the existence of the subconscious only by going beyond strict empiricism to use the same type of reasoning that we rely on to prove the existence of God.

The resulting truth is just as "real" as any that is established in the lab. The opportunity for Thomas to touch the wounds in the body of Jesus made the resurrection no more of a reality than it would have been otherwise. That is why the Lord said to Thomas, "Because you have seen me, you have believed; blessed are those who have not seen and yet have believed" (John 20:29).

We must note, however, that Jesus understood the power of empirical skepticism. He did not reproach Thomas for his doubt. Instead, He responded to this effect: "Thomas, I understand that you have some questions. Let me see if I can answer them for you." Three years earlier He had dealt with Nathaniel's skepticism the same way when, in John 1, the young man professed disbelief that "anything good could come out of Nazareth."

We have much to learn from the way that Jesus reacted to Thomas and Nathaniel. We might be intimidated, or at least left uncomfortable, by such straight-forward challenges to what we believe.

But not Jesus. He never ducked an honest question. He ducked a number of dishonest ones. But never an honest question. He never feared the man who was honest and forthright about his doubts. Indeed, He found such men among the most teachable on earth.

Four types of doubt, then, have presented themselves in John 20: emotional skepticism, dispositional skepticism, practical skepticism, and empirical skepticism. And which of them presents the greatest threat to the church today?

If I were to hazard a guess, I would argue that practical skepticism is our most serious problem — a practical skepticism which leaves Christian lives without a consistent, powerful witness. A friend of mine attributes our enfeebled witness to the problem of Sadduceeism in the church. The Sadducees, you recall, did not believe in the resurrection.

We would hardly allow ourselves to deny the resurrection openly the way the Sadducees did. But we can give lip service to the resurrection while failing to really believe in it. Christianity can become for us a type of "fire insurance," providing protection in case there is an afterlife. But just in case this world is all there is, we want to enjoy its allurements as much as our conscience will allow.

Consequently, we can find ourselves living with one foot in the eternal realm, the other planted in the temporal. And then we cannot understand why we experience such inner conflict, why our lives possess so little of that peace which passes understanding. Like those cowering disciples in that locked room, we need to hear the Lord's repeated blessing, "Peace be with you."

And when that peace takes control of our life, the practical effects can be both sudden and dramatic. Within two months, those once fearful disciples were testifying with boldness about the risen Lord whom they served. No longer were they wringing their hands, bemoaning what the world was coming to. Instead, they were holding their hands high in victory, announcing the good news of what had come to the world.

May we, too, shake off our practical skepticism. May we gain that genuine peace that comes with the knowledge of the resurrection. And may we, in the power of that knowledge, take the message of a risen Lord to a world which perishes without Him.

12

Things Broken,
Too Broke to Mend

JOE SCHUBERT

The days after the death of our Lord are described in the first eight verses of the last chapter of Mark. When the Sabbath was over, Mary Magdalene, Mary the mother of James, and Salome bought spices with which to anoint Jesus' body. Very early on the first day of the week, just after sunrise, they were on their way to the tomb. They asked each other as they walked, "Who will roll the stone away from the entrance of the tomb?" But when they looked up, they saw that the large stone had been rolled away. As they entered the tomb, they saw a young man, dressed in a white robe, sitting on the right side. They became frightened. "Don't be alarmed," he said. "You are looking for Jesus the Nazarene, who was crucified. He has risen! He is not here. See the place where they laid Him. But go, tell His disciples and Peter, 'He is going ahead of you into Galilee. There you will see Him, just as He told you.'" Trembling and bewildered, the women fled from the tomb. They said nothing to anyone because of fear.

In an old poem, "The Widow in the By Street," John Masefield depicts a scene of dramatic agony. A young man is about to be executed by the state for crimes he has committed. He is going to be executed by a hanging. In the crowd to witness the final event is his mother. As the trap door was opened and the rope did its work, the mother fell crumpled to the ground and began to sob. Those who stood nearby heard her saying something about "things broken, too broke to mend." Part of this woman's anguish, no doubt, was her memory of her past failures as a mother and her sense of shame at this failure being witnessed by the world. But also a part of that anguish, undoubtedly, was linked to the future. She now was left all alone in the world, without a husband and without a son. She believed there was really nothing to live for. There was no future, no hope. There was only a deep, foreboding sense of despair. There were "things broken, too broke to mend."

That phrase is an awesome one, for it suggests nothing to live for, no sense of promise ahead. As I understand it, this is the very essence of despair. It is to find yourself at a certain point in life where there is a past, there is a present, but there is no future. There is nothing at all to look forward to.

I. The Disciples' Despair

It is interesting to note the parallels between Masefield's poem and the circumstances that surrounded the death of Jesus. In the poem a young man is being executed by the state in the presence of his mother. When Jesus died that Friday afternoon at 3 o'clock, the hopes of hundreds of people died with Him. They had believed He was the Messiah. Ever since He had begun teaching in Galilee and had done His mighty works in Palestine, the word had spread rapidly that He indeed was the long-awaited Deliverer of Israel. The common people began to stir with hope and excitement. But then, just as quickly as His popularity had risen, the tide had turned against Him. Before most of the people had realized what was really happening, there He was, another convicted felon in the crucifixion annals of Rome.

The poem talks about "things broken, too broke to mend." This had to be the mood of His followers that Friday afternoon as they hurriedly laid His body in the borrowed tomb before the sun went down. More than one woman crumpled to the ground in tears that night. At the point when they had come to expect so much, suddenly it was all over. That Saturday after the death of Jesus must have been the darkest day the disciples of Jesus had ever spent. What Jerusalem and Rome had succeeded in breaking seemed for all the world too broken to mend.

II. The Surprise on Sunday

But, then, as Mark tells us, the absolutely unexpected happened. Early on Sunday morning, a group of women made their way to the tomb to finish anointing the body of Jesus. They were worried about getting the great stone rolled away from the entrance of the tomb. Scholars suggest that the stone might have weighed as much as one thousand pounds. This enormous problem did not occur to them until they had almost arrived at the tomb. But when they arrived, they saw that the problem had already been solved. The heavy stone had already been moved away.

They also found that the tomb was empty. At first they believed that this was simply another tragedy in their long list of catastrophes. It did not occur to them that this was something God had done. They assumed, as any Palestinian would have in the first century, that grave robbers had robbed the tomb and further desecrated the body.

Matthew tells us how that stone happened to be already moved when the women arrived. Matthew 28:2-4 says, "There was a violent earthquake, for an angel of the Lord came down from heaven and, going to the tomb, rolled back the stone and sat on it. His appearance was like lightning, and his clothes were white as snow. The guards were so afraid of him that they shook and became like dead men." All of this had happened a short time before the women had arrived. By the time the women arrived, the guards were apparently gone. The tomb was now completely empty, except for a young man. The gospels tell us the young man was an angel. He said, "Do not be afraid, for I know that you are looking for Jesus, who was crucified. He is not here; He has risen, just as He said. Come and see the place where He lay." Then all of the events began to fall into place. Jesus was not dead any longer. The body that had been killed on Friday had been raised back to life on Sunday. The empty tomb was not the work of grave robbers; it was the work of God Himself. They could hardly grasp it. Jesus was alive and back in the world! The angel also said, "Then go quickly and tell His disciples: 'He has risen from the dead and is going ahead of you into Galilee. There you will see Him.' Now I have told you" (v. 7).

III. God's Grace

Why do you suppose the angel singled out Peter as one who was particularly to be told this message? It was done because just three days prior to this Peter denied that he had had any association with the Lord. This underscored the fact that, although Peter had rejected Jesus, Jesus had not rejected him.

The same was true of all the disciples. On the night of Jesus' betrayal the other apostles did basically what Peter did. All the rest forsook Him and refused to stand by Him. They left and fled in fear for their own lives. But on the heels of the resurrection is the affirmation that though the disciples had abandoned Him, He was not abandoning them. In the face of the denial, the betrayal, and even the crucifixion, God was saying, "I am not giving up on these men. Furthermore, I am not giving up on the world." What they had thought was over and done with, a thing broken, too broken to mend, was still very much alive. This sudden realization had turned things around for those disciples; it had given them a whole new perspective on life. The resurrection of Jesus reminded these people all over again that God is a factor to be reckoned with when one thinks about the future.

This is something we so easily forget in the hustle and bustle of life. You and I tend to look at events horizontally, as if our own wisdom, knowledge, and energy are all of the forces operating in this world. We have concluded that if we cannot figure out how to accomplish something with our own power and intelligence, then it simply cannot be accomplished. We are like those women who were worrying about who was going to roll away the stone. They knew of a challenge which was beyond their ability and capacity to solve. But when they arrived it had already been done.

God, too, plays a part in what is possible and impossible in the future. God has both power and mercy beyond anything we can imagine. In Romans 4:17, Paul refers to God as a God who gives life to the dead and calls into existence things that do not exist. God was able to take a dead body, one out of which all the vitality had gone, and bring that body back to life. Paul infers in Romans 4 that this is akin to what God did when He took things that did not exist and spoke them into existence by the word of power. This is the ultimate as far as power is concerned. It changes forever the way we look at the words *possible* and *impossible*. What problem is really too deep or too complex for a God who is both

Creator and Resurrector? If God was able to raise Jesus Christ from the dead, what stone in our lives today is He powerless to move?

How great, in my opinion, is it that God should have even wanted to raise Jesus, in view of how the world had just treated His Son! The mercy and patience expressed in the resurrection of Christ are beyond my comprehension. Jesus represented God's last and best effort to do something about this rebellious planet. Almost as soon as the first sin on the earth occurred, God set about to redeem man from his sin. God spoke to Abraham, Isaac, Jacob, and their descendants and revealed to them His will. Later He sent the Law, the prophets, and the priests. The roll call of God's efforts was a long one. The cross was the climactic attempt. It was as though He was saying, "This is My Son, one like Myself. Surely you will listen to Him." At first this Son was treated with warm affection. Then, the same world that had stoned the prophets and had broken the Law turned on the Son. In the end He was utterly rejected, tortured, and finally put to death.

Only a sensitive parent can begin to understand how God must have felt on that Friday afternoon. Use your imagination! Suppose that you become aware of a family in your area that really needs help. You decide to do what you can to help them. You secure a job for the man, give them a place to live, and do whatever is in your power to meet the other needs of this family. But the needs grow worse. The parents refuse to work. They tear up the place in which they live. Realizing the task is a larger one than you had bargained for, you call in social workers, and you call in the county agencies. But the family refuses all offers of assistance. One day your only son says, "Let me try to help this family. In view of all that you have tried to do for them, and in view of the fact that I am your son, maybe they will listen to me." The son goes to see the family, but instead of just running him off as they had done with the others who had tried to help, they tie him to a chair, torture him, and kill him in cold blood. What would your attitude be? Would you mark off this family as worthless and hopeless? Of course you would. And yet, can you believe that by bringing Christ back from the grave, God said once again, "These people who have rejected every overture I have made still have a future. I am going to try again to reach them."

By calling for the disciples and Peter to meet Him in Galilee, God manifested a mercy, a patience, and a hope that is absolutely unbelievable. This is the God we must reckon with as we contemplate the future. Who are we to look upon our broken things and say they are too broken to mend? If God was able and willing to take the broken body of Jesus and bring it back to life, what can He not mend in our lives?

IV. Hope for the Hopeless

One of the great sermons of a previous generation is by Carlyle Marney; it is titled "God's Strong Hand." It was about Judas and the ultimate tragedy of his life. His undoing, according to Marney, was not the fact that he betrayed Jesus, but the fact that he did not stay around long enough to see what God can do with human defects. In other words, Judas' sin was the sin of despair. When the full impact of what he had done finally hit him, it was more than he could stand. It seemed to him a thing too broken to mend. He saw himself as someone without any redemptive quality at all, a creature so contemptible that he was utterly beyond mercy. Therefore, he took his own life. But what a pity, what a pity!

If Judas could only have waited until that Sunday morning when God raised Jesus from the grave, then, undoubtedly, he could have heard that the angel proclaimed to the women, "He is not here. He is going ahead into Galilee. Go tell the disciples, Peter *and Judas.*" What Judas did was not a great deal worse than what Peter did. What Peter did was not a great deal worse than what the disciples did. Enough mercy existed even for Judas.

Do you have in your life things which seem broken — hopes, health, a marriage? For some of you the future may look very bleak. The future is nothing but a lot of gray stones for you to move. Listen, there is also God. He is a factor to be reckoned with. In God there is power enough and mercy enough to deal with whatever brokenness you have. With God, no broken thing is too broken to mend. This is the message of the resurrection.

It is impressing to me to consider the number of Scriptures in the New Testament that link together the power of God that raised Jesus from the dead and the power that God is willing to exercise through our bodies as His people today. In Ephesians 1:18-20, Paul writes:

> I pray also that the eyes of your heart may be
> enlightened in order that you may know the hope to
> which He has called you, the riches of His glorious
> inheritance in the saints, and His incomparably great
> power for us who believe. That power is like the working

of His mighty strength, which He exerted in Christ
when He raised Him from the dead and seated Him
at His right hand in the heavenly realms.

Romans 8:11 says, "And if the Spirit of Him who raised Jesus from the dead is living in you, He who raised Christ from the dead will also give life to your mortal bodies through His Spirit, who lives in you." And Romans 6:3, 4 says, "Or don't you know that all of us who were baptized into Christ Jesus were baptized into His death? We were therefore buried with Him through baptism into death in order that, just as Christ was raised from the dead through the glory of the Father, we too may live a new life."

Conclusion

The difference between despair and hope is God. The difference between frustration and fulfillment is God. The difference between the death of Jesus on Friday and the resurrection of Jesus on Sunday is God. The difference between the old life of failure and sin and the new life of victory and power is God. There is power for you; there is mercy for you; there is forgiveness for you if you are willing to give your life to Him.

13

Reaching Modern Man with the Risen Lord

AVON MALONE

> Because if thou shalt confess with thy mouth Jesus as
> Lord and shalt believe in thy heart that God raised
> Him from the dead, thou shalt be saved . . .
>
> (Romans 10:9).

Bernard Ramm has said that the resurrection is *the* miracle of the New Testament. With this overstatement he seeks to emphasize that the resurrection is central to Christianity. It is crucial to its claims. In I Corinthians 15, Paul affirms that the resurrection is the great capstone of evidence upon which the whole system rests. If this foundation can be proven false, the system crumbles. Paul sees too, quite clearly in this context, that the future resurrection of believers is linked inextricably with the resurrection of Jesus Christ. Inseparably bound up together, if He was raised, then they will be raised.

> Now if Christ is preached that He hath been raised
> from the dead, how say some among you that there
> is no resurrection of the dead? But if there is no
> resurrection of the dead, neither hath Christ been
> raised: and if Christ hath not been raised, then is our
> preaching vain, your faith also is vain. Yea, and we are
> found false witnesses of God; because we witness of
> God that He raised up Christ: whom He raised not
> up, if so be that the dead are not raised. For if the dead

are not raised, neither hath Christ been raised: and
if Christ hath not been raised, your faith is vain; ye
are yet in your sins. Then they also that are fallen asleep
in Christ have perished. If we have only hoped in Christ
in this life, we are of all men most pitiable (I Corinthians
15:12-19).

The preaching is vain if Christ be not raised. It is empty, devoid
of power and saving content. If He is not raised, your faith is vain. For
your faith, if properly focused and founded, is in a living and risen Christ.

In Romans 4:25 Paul said, "He was delivered up for our trespasses
and raised for our justification." The court term "justification" means
acquittal; to be rendered guiltless. Once I was conversing with Frank
Pack. He said, "Here is something that has helped me, and I have used
it in my preaching. Justified means 'just as if I had never sinned.' " That
is exactly what it means. Paul said He was raised for our justification.
If He was not raised, we have not been justified.

. . . few, that is, eight souls, were saved through water:
which also after a true likeness doth now save you,
even baptism, not the putting away of the filth of the
flesh, but the interrogation of a good conscience toward
God, through the resurrection of Jesus Christ (I Peter
3:20, 21).

Peter is saying baptism saves us by the resurrection of Jesus Christ.
If Christ has not been raised, baptism does not save us.

But if He was raised, baptism saves by the resurrection of Jesus Christ.
We are talking about *the* miracle of the Bible. Look at His claims: "I
am the bread of life" (John 6:35); "I am the light of the world" (John
8:12); "I am the resurrection, and the life" (John 11:25f). In John 10:30
he said, "I and the Father are one." Let me tell you something. If Christ
has been raised, all those claims are true. If Christ has been raised, the
Old Testament is true and the New Testament is true. He endorses one
and authorizes the other. He stands between those covenants. He puts
His stamp of approval on the Law of Moses and the prophets and the
psalms (Luke 24:44). Do you see the consequences of the resurrection?

Somebody says they may be able to believe in Jesus, but they have
difficulty in believing the early chapters of Genesis. In Matthew 19 they

ask, "Can a man put away his wife for every cause?" Jesus responds, "Have you not read that He that made them at the beginning made them male and female; and, therefore, shall a man leave his father and mother and cleave to his wife, and the two shall be one flesh . . ." That looks back to the early chapters of Genesis (cf. Genesis 2:24). Old and New Testaments are validated by the worth of this one who has been raised (cf. John 10:34, 35). His great claims are true!

Christianity does not hang from a skyhook. We are not Christians because of personal subjective experiences. Christianity is not validated when we talk to an unbeliever on the basis of subjective experiences. It is not a mere philosophy; it is not a mere ethic. God left His mark in the bone and blood and body of history. Our faith in Jesus Christ and the resurrection rests upon historical evidence. We have at our disposal authentic, historical evidence from which we may form a conclusion about the nature and the claims, work, person, and power of the Lord Jesus Christ.

Jesus is a real historical person, and informed unbelievers do not make the effort today to deny the historicity of Jesus because it cannot be done. Uninspired writers — Tacitus, Suetonius, Josephus, the little-known Thallus —all attest to Jesus' historicity. No one can deny the historical reality, the actual existence of Jesus of Nazareth.

He lived, He died, He was buried in the tomb of Joseph of Arimathea — and that tomb was found empty. Friend and foe alike must admit these facts of history. F. F. Bruce, the eminent British biblical scholar, has written a book, *The New Testament Documents, Are They Reliable?* And Bruce answers with an emphatic "yes." The documents telling of Jesus are reliable. In the book *The Divine Demonstration*, H. Everest makes this completely clear. Everest argues that when we look at the New Testament documents, we are looking at works that are authentic, credible and were circulated early among the churches. We have over 5,000 pieces of manuscript evidence for the text of the New Testament. There are the great manuscripts going back to the fourth century, with some fragments going back to early in the second century. Everest shows that in addition to the manuscripts, there is an unbroken succession of quotations in the Christian writers: Augustine in the fourth century; Origin in the third; Tertullian, Irenaeus, and Justin Martyr in the second; and Hermas, Barnabas, Polycarp, and others who write in the last half of the first century. All of these writers and many others bear testimony to the authenticity of the New Testament documents.

The New Testament writers were either deceived or deceivers, or they wrote the truth. The first two alternatives are clearly inadequate. They walked with Him; they talked with Him. Their doubts were dispelled. They were not deceived. And these simple Galileans who died for their testimony were not deceivers. We have reliable historical evidence from eyewitnesses. They wrote the truth! These men were persecuted for what they insisted upon as being the truth. Even to death they insisted that He had been raised!

Look carefully at their accounts. Matthew, like so many of the writers, tells us about Mary Magdalene and the other Mary. Matthew tells us that the Jewish rulers were apprehensive and so the guards were bribed to tell that "the disciples took the body while we slept." Alexander Campbell pointed out that there is no contemporaneous evidence denying the resurrection save that which has a lie stamped upon its forehead: "The disciples stole the body while we slept." When have sleeping men been reliable witnesses to what took place during their slumber? It was something they were bribed to say and they knew it was not true. Interestingly, Matthew faithfully records the lie the guards were bribed to tell.

When various ones — the men who had seen Him on the way to Emmaus, the women who were last at the cross and first at the tomb — began to noise abroad what they had seen, do you know what some of the initial reactions were? Unbelief, doubt, fear. They were not expecting what happened. Many of the theories of the unbelievers — "hallucination," "optical illusion," etc. — rested on the premise that a high degree of expectancy prevailed among the disciples. That is not the picture painted in the gospels. They are surprised, disturbed, afraid, perplexed as the women came saying the tomb was empty. All of this actually makes the evidence even stronger.

In John 20, Mary Magdalene goes and finds the tomb empty. She lets Peter and John know what she has found. If you were choosing men for a track team, you would pick John before Peter. But if you want somebody who will just blare in there, Peter is the man. So there is a little foot race that goes on and John is faster afoot. However, when Peter gets there, he rushes right in. They found the burial clothes, not in disarray or confusion, but "lying, and the napkin, that was upon his head, not lying with the linen cloths, but rolled up in a place by itself " (John 20:6, 7). John entered and he saw and he believed (John 20:8). He may have been the first one to be convinced. John is already beginning to see that no one took the body away. Grave robbers would not leave the scene like that.

Later in the same chapter, the sceptical Thomas is himself completely convinced. Don't miss an assembly on the first day of the week, because you may miss something wonderful. That is what happened to Thomas. They were behind locked doors and Jesus appeared. Thomas was not there. He missed it. When told that Jesus had appeared, Thomas said (if it might be phrased in 20th century speech), "I will have to have empirical evidence, or I won't believe." The next Sunday Jesus came and confronted him with exactly that kind of evidence: the nail-pierced hands; the sword-torn side. The cry of Thomas is the crescendo of John's gospel: "My Lord and my God" (John 20:24-28). All doubt is dissipated like dew before the sun — He has been raised.

L. R. Wilson in his book *The Triumphant Lord* imagines the situation in which a presidential candidate who expects victory tells a dozen people: "I have places in my cabinet for you, and sometime between my election and my inauguration I am going to see you, and we will work these things out." He is elected. Immediately after the election the news is flashed out that his whereabouts are unknown. Suddenly two women come in with some news that might indicate something about him. Then two men come in and say they have dined with him. Next he appears to a dozen people. And then he stands before a larger group, some 500, and he makes a speech. Finally he comes back to that smaller group and he gives them a charge or commission. He gives them the necessary credentials to serve as his cabinet officers, and after that time no one doubts that they have seen this particular candidate. They proceed to do their work decisively and dynamically. Under those exact circumstances, who would question the fact that the inner circle or the 500 had seen him? We have from the New Testament documents reliable evidence of this kind.

Hear Jesus: "Handle me, and see; for a spirit hath not flesh and bones, as ye behold me having" (Luke 24:39). He insists that His bodily resurrection was real; they were not seeing a ghost. John can write: "That which was from the beginning, that which we have heard, that which we have seen with our eyes, that which we beheld, and our hands handled, concerning the word of life" (I John 1:1). Christianity is not some vague, nebulous philosophy built upon some profound proposition. It is rooted in history.

Phillip Schaff, a renowned church historian, has said that "a self-invented falsehood could not give them the courage and the constancy of faith for the proclamation of the resurrection at the peril of their lives." That is, ordinarily men will not die for a lie. Years ago, as an undergraduate student, I wrote a paper on "Theories Concerning the Resurrection" (the swoon theory, the optical illusion theory, etc.). Question: why were these theories formed in the first place? *The tomb was empty!* No need for theories otherwise.

What happened to the body? What are the possibilities? (1) The foes took it or (2) The friends took it or (3) He was raised by the power of God. As L. R. Wilson has written, there is not any point in the foes taking it because that is the very thing they were seeking to prevent. They already had the body. It was under heavy Roman guard. If the foes had the body, they could have stopped the preaching in Acts 2 by just unveiling the corpse of Christ. The foes of the faith did not take the body. What about the friends of our Lord? Did they move or take the body? As stressed earlier, how could such a self-invented falsehood give rise to the change in these disciples? How could such fraud produce the fearlessness that was later seen in their lives? Earlier, they turned from Him disillusioned, disheartened, still not completely understanding the nature of the kingdom. They saw their hopes crumble on the execution hill known as Golgotha, and then suddenly it was all changed. What caused the change? The resurrection!

Peter can write in I Peter 1:3: "who according to His great mercy begat us again unto a living hope by the resurrection of Jesus Christ from the dead." Only an empty tomb and a miraculous resurrection could account for the powerful proclamation on Pentecost:

> Ye men of Israel, hear these words: Jesus of Nazareth, a man approved of God unto you by mighty works and wonders and signs which God did by Him in the midst of you, even as ye yourselves know; Him, being delivered up by the determinate council and foreknowledge of God, ye by the hand of lawless men did crucify and slay: whom God raised up, having loosed the pangs of death, because it was not possible that He should be holden of it (Acts 2:22-24).
>
> Brethren, I may say unto you freely of the patriarch David, that he both died and was buried, and his tomb is with us unto this day. Being therefore a prophet, and

> knowing that God has sworn with an oath to him,
> that of the fruit of his loins he would set one upon
> his throne; he foreseeing this spake of the resurrection
> of Christ, that neither was he left unto Hades, nor did
> his flesh see corruption. This Jesus did God raise up,
> whereof we all are witnesses (Acts 2:29-320.

Look at the arch persecutor — Saul of Tarsus — now Paul, the peerless apostle to Gentiles. What caused the change? The resurrection. From fanaticism to faith is Paul's story, and only the resurrection of our Lord can account for that.

The conversion of Saul, the very existence of the church, the remarkable change that took place in disheartened and disillusioned disciples and apostles of our Lord. All this and more is best accounted for by the resurrection of Jesus.

A good working hypothesis is to take the simplest explanation and try that out and see if it will fit the data. Here we have the change, here we have the existence of the church, here we have undeniably the empty tomb. We are left with but one conclusion. He was declared to be the Son of God with power by the resurrection from the dead. Friend, if Christ has been raised, then the darkest, bleakest, blackest day of your life can be a day of hope. It can be a day in which you can do battle with the evil one knowing resources that are not your own.

When G. C. Brewer was near death, he confided to friends that poems, illustrations, and other figures of speech he had often used in preaching were not really a source of comfort at all. He was asked, "Brother Brewer, what is a source of comfort?" And he answered, "The resurrection of Jesus Christ." He has been raised! And that makes all the difference in the world. That is a place to stand, something that is real and can help us in time and throughout eternity. "Up from the grave He arose with a might triumph o'er His foes." Convinced by the evidence, may we all exclaim with Thomas, "My Lord and my God."

14

The Life of Christ from a New Dimension

RANDY MAYEUX

She was bright, articulate, energetic — depressed. For years she had struggled with the shallowness of her church experience. She longed for a deeper, more life-shaping faith. She prayed, read His word, trusted. But she needed more help. And her church was simply not providing it.

She knew the answer. It is an ancient answer. It is a simple answer. Yet our complex lives continually ignore the simple, the obvious. The catalyst for our luncheon appointment was her own spiritual desperation. Just the Sunday before, the sermon had been on the teaching method of Christ. It carefully examined how He taught, and some of what He taught. But it was all so distant from real life. There was no attempt to bridge to her daily struggles. And then came the penetrating lines. She asked: "Why do we view Christ as though the entirety of His life was a brief 33-year span some 2,000 years ago? He was alive long before that. He is alive today! Why are we so oblivious to, so threatened by, the contemporary life of Christ?"

It was a penetrating question — one that drove me to my study; one that launched an entire series of sermons on living life on a new dimension. And at the center of this new dimension is the life-changing, life-shaping realization that He is alive — living and moving among us — today.

How Do We Usually View Christ?

We know so much about our Master. We know Him as a teacher who taught with great content. Nicodemus recognized this about Him: "Rabbi, we know that you are a teacher who has come from God" (John 3:2). And it is helpful to go back, let His words shape our understanding of God, of our own situation — to shape our worldview.

We also know Him as a good man who set a good example — a God-like example. At one point, He performed the menial task of washing the dirty feet of His followers. He instructed: "I have set you an example that you should do as I have done for you" (John 13:15). Peter was one of the ones who had his feet washed, and he never forgot the compelling power of the example of Christ. Years later, in encouraging fellow believers to stand firm, with love, in the midst of suffering, he reminded them of the example of Christ: "To this you were called, because Christ has suffered for you, leaving you an example, that you should follow in His steps . . . When they hurled their insults at Him, He did not retaliate . . . Instead, He entrusted Himself to Him who judges justly" (I Peter 2:21-23).

We also know Jesus as the one who, in one great act of selfless sacrifice, purchased for us our eternal salvation. Paul used the Old Testament imagery and stated that "God presented Him as a sacrifice of atonement" (Romans 3:25). His death, a very real death at a specific moment of history, secured the forgiveness of all of our sins.

But we fall short with such understanding. We tend to think of Him as one who was raised from the dead, gave a few final instructions, and then "retired" for an eternity of rest in heaven.

I recently sat at lunch with a professor at USC. She was asking perplexing questions about the problem of suffering and evil. She asked me directly: "Do you believe God is active at all in today's world? Do you pray expecting something to happen?" This is the same question that my earlier encounter raised, and it points out the dimension that is missing.

What's Missing?

To view Christ as just a teacher who taught, and not one who now teaches, is to believe only in an ancient historical figure. To view Christ as one who set an example, even with the ultimate example of His own sacrifice, is "nice" — but it too is inadequate.

We simply must view Christ as our contemporary. His call to mission (Matthew 28:18-20) comes with an astounding promise: "I will be with you."

Not — "the memory of Christ will be with you," but He will be with you. He has promised to be present with every believer throughout history. The Bible affirms this promise again and again. For example:

"I tell you the truth, anyone who has faith in me will do what I have been doing. He will do even greater things than these, because I am going to the Father" (John 14:12).

"Christ in you (is) the hope of glory" (Colossians 1:27).

"I no longer live, but Christ lives in me" (Galatians 2:20).

It is no wonder that Paul was ready to cast all to the rubbish heap, leaving only his one driving passion: "I want to know Christ."

He promises to give us His powerful presence today. To study the life of Christ is not a study in ancient history, but to become a part of a life and mission that transcends time. We do not worship a dead hero, but we are partners with a resurrected Lord, who is even now at work among us and through us.

Looking at the Life of Christ from a New Dimension

This view opens up entire new vistas to us. We start looking for Christ before Bethlehem.

"In the beginning was the Word," wrote John, and so we look for Him from the very beginning. When we do, then it is no mystery why Moses chose to be mistreated, for "he regarded disgrace for the sake of Christ (not God, but Christ) as of greater value than the treasures of Egypt" (Hebrews 11:25-26). If the writer of Hebrews could find Christ in the life of Moses, we too can look for His presence throughout the Old Testament.

And you keep going forward from Bethlehem, past Jerusalem, past the times of the apostles. He is no retired martyr. He has been actively involved in the lives of His people throughout the centuries. If you want to look at the dramatic, look at the study done by Martin Luther, the preaching done by John Wesley, the teaching done by Alexander Campbell. Or if you want to look at the more "commonplace," yet just as real, activity of Christ, then remember the way that Francis of Assisi washed the open sores of lepers, or remember how Dr. Jerry Mays left the United States with his family to build a hospital in Tanzania, named Chimala Mission. You could write your own list, from history, and from personal observation. You know that He is alive and active today. You've seen Him! You've even felt His power in your life.

The Key — A Right View of the Resurrection

The presence of Christ in our midst today is the direct result of the truth of the resurrection. A few years ago, Landon Saunders was speaking to a group of college students in Colorado. He was speaking the words of the gospel, noting that Jesus died for our sins, was buried, and then was raised from the dead. At that point, a foreign student interrupted him. "Pardon me, sir. Are you saying that this Jesus physically died, and literally, physically came back to life?" After getting over the shock of someone interrupting a sermon, Landon responded: "Yes, that's what I said. And that's what I believe is true." The student continued the dialogue: "Then that means that He is alive today, doesn't it?" Landon said, "Yes." The student then said: "Then that means we can meet Him and know Him today, doesn't it?"

That is the truth of the gospel. The gospel is not just "Jesus died, was buried, and was raised from the dead." This is an incomplete gospel. We as a people are known as particular in our study of the word of God. We want to include all teaching (e.g., not "repent," but "repent and be baptized"). This is as it should be. If so, then note Paul's full description of the gospel:

I want to remind you of the gospel . . . By this gospel you are saved . . . For what I received I passed on to you as of first importance. That Christ died for our sins, according to the Scriptures, that He was buried, that He was raised on the third day, according to the Scriptures, and that He appeared to Peter . . . to the twelve . . . to more than five hundred . . . and last of all, He appeared to me also" (I Corinthians 15:1-8).

Paul's description of the gospel includes the appearances of Jesus. Not just that He was raised, but that "He appeared, and I've seen Him — I've met Him!"

This truth is the central truth that sets Christianity apart. The resurrection means that we can (we should, we must) know Him today. We too have met this resurrected Lord.

84

So What?

Since He is alive today, and you can know Him today, this sets an agenda for your Christian life.

Concern –1 — You need to carefully cultivate a closeness to Him. Paul prayed for it, for Himself and others: "I want to know Christ" (Philippians 3:10). "I pray that He may strengthen you with power through His Spirit in your inner being, so that Christ may dwell in your hearts through faith" (Ephesians 3:16-17).

Such ancient disciplines as reading the Bible, and prayer, have always been the most basic avenues to develop closeness to Christ. The experienced wisdom of the ages should be followed. Develop and deepen these life-shaping, Christ-knowing disciplines.

I remember my days as a student at Pepperdine University. Many great moments stand out as highlights. But one teacher had a personal touch that was unforgettable.

Dr. Frank Pack taught the more "biblical" classes. These classes had the potential of becoming very "ivory tower" — simply academic, with no concern for "real life." But Dr. Pack would begin each class with a prayer. And he would always find a moment to slip in a story about a real life "ministry situation." It was clear that Bible study, for him, was no mere academic pursuit. It was the discipline that shaped his heart and his life. He knew God intimately — and that relationship drove him to a life of servanthood — a life of genuine ministry. Which leads me to . . .

Concern –2 — We need to better understand Christian ministry. To draw close to Christ is to lose yourself in His concerns. He will do through you what He did while on earth in the flesh, and what He has done and will do through countless numbers of followers throughout history. Such activities as ministry to the poor, sharing the wonderful message of good news, acting as peacemakers, and many others are tasks that unleash the presence of Christ in your own life.

In your own ministry, you experience a paradox — Christ is ministering through you, and you are ministering to Christ. "I no longer live, but Christ lives through me," stated Paul (Galatians 2:20). And Jesus described that whenever a believer feeds a hungry person, clothes a cold person, even provides friendship to a stranger, then in reality the believer is ministering to Christ Himself! "I tell you the truth, whatever you did for one of the least of these brothers of mine, you did for me" (Matthew 25:40).

Since Christ truly is alive today, with all of His power available, then we realize that the new birth is no myth. People that we label "hopeless" are, in fact, able to be changed by His power.

Look for Him

Therefore, let us respond to the call to look for Him — expectantly — with a heart ready to receive His presence. If we do, He will come!

The young lady was right. It is such a shallow, false view to define the life of Christ as something that "happened." The life of Christ continues — through today, on into the future.

And so we too can say, with certainty, that: "We want to know Christ and the power of His resurrection and the fellowship of sharing in His sufferings." — "Come, Lord Jesus." To us. Again. Today!

15

The Man Who Took a Chance

GAYLE CROWE

The *Odyssey* is an ancient Greek tale about the wanderings of its hero, Odysseus, in the years after the fall of Troy. As the story develops, whenever Odysseus was away from home he entrusted his son, Telemachus, to his friend, Mentor. Over the years a strong friendship grew between the older Mentor and the younger Telemachus; Mentor became the boy's guardian, teacher, and father figure.

To this day, a mentor — or the lack of one — can be crucial to one's success. A mentor is anyone of influence or knowledge who takes the time to give help and encouragement to someone younger or less knowledgeable. In the book *Mentors and Proteges*, Phillips-Jones suggests that many people can point back to one or two individuals who gave them direction and encouragement at a crucial time.

Aristotle, for example, openly acknowledged his debt to his teacher, Plato. Michelangelo had the guidance of his mentor, Leonardo da Vinci. The urging of Robert Schumann inspired Brahms to compose as he did. Carl Jung learned at the feet of Sigmund Freud. Coming closer to today, Dick Cavett had his Jack Paar. And where would Joe Namath have been without the coaching of Bear Bryant?

How refreshing when someone older and more experienced is willing to take a novice under his wing! Whether the lessons taught relate to matters of career, academics, social graces, or the spiritual dimension of life, the guidance of one older and wiser should always be appreciated.

Barnabas, the Encourager

The fourth chapter of Acts introduces such a person. He is not called a mentor, but even his very name captures the essence of a mentor's role.

Joseph, a Levite from Cyprus, whom the apostles called Barnabas (which means The Encourager), sold a field he owned and brought the money and put it at the apostles' feet (4:36-37).

How the need for funds arose is not known; the man from Cyprus simply saw the plight of people in a desperate situation and rose to the occasion with his own resources. Evidently the apostles detected in this act something unusual about this man Joseph and gave him a special name: Barnabas, The Encourager. As events developed, they were right in their early judgment about him.

The next time the writer of Acts mentions Barnabas is during the days immediately after the conversion of Saul of Tarsus. As told in Acts 9, Saul was confronted by the Lord on the road to Damascus. Faced with the fact that he was clearly wrong in his judgment of Jesus of Nazareth, he was sent into the city to await instructions. Three days later Saul was baptized and almost immediately began a preaching mission in Damascus. So successful was he in his mission that the Jewish leaders in that city conspired to kill him.

Leaving Damascus behind, he went on to Jerusalem where he hoped for a cordial reception from fellow-Christians who would realize that he could be a great asset in their work. When he arrived, however, he was given a cool reception by a wary and suspicious church. The text says, "They were all afraid of him, not believing that he really was an apostle" (9:26). Why not! This man had earned his reputation by arresting Christians and carting them off for trial and imprisonment. His intention, as he himself acknowledged later to the Galatians, had been to try to destroy the church. Small wonder that the leaders of the church in Jerusalem immediately took a "hands-off" posture toward Saul.

Now enters Barnabas into the picture. The Encourager took a personal risk. He took Saul to meet with the apostles. Acting as the intermediary, he told them how Saul on his journey had seen the Lord, how the Lord had spoken to him, and how in Damascus he had spoken fearlessly in the name of Jesus.

Why did Barnabas go out on a limb for Saul? Had he been with Saul in Damascus? Had he heard of Saul's work there from a reliable third party? No one knows, except that what he did was consistent with his character. True to his name, he saw Saul as one who needed encouragement. As a brother in Christ, Barnabas sponsored Saul at a crucial time in Saul's Christian life and ministry. With his help, Saul was "in" — instantly a part of the inner circle of church leaders in Jerusalem. Acts 9:28 states, "So Saul stayed with them and moved about freely in Jerusalem, speaking boldly in the name of the Lord." The picture of Barnabas is consistent: both Acts 4 and Acts 9 agree that Barnabas was on the scene, he was lending a hand, he was ministering to people who needed encouraging.

The Encouragement Widens

Just as Barnabas was trusting of Saul, he was also trusted by others. The next time he is found in Acts he is again in the conciliator role. The church in Jerusalem heard about the fast-growing and dynamic church in Antioch, and apparently some in Jerusalem were cautious: "Something's wrong there! Why is that such a fast-growing church? Are they holding to the doctrine in their great move to evangelize?" They decided to send an ambassador up to Antioch to see what was happening, and who should they decide to send but The Encourager, Barnabas. Acts 11:23 reports, "When he arrived and saw the evidence of the grace of God, he was glad and encouraged them all to remain true to the Lord with all their hearts." Others might have returned to Jerusalem with raised eyebrows claiming to have found the wrong for which they went looking. Not so with Barnabas; he came, analyzed the situation, and endorsed the work in Antioch with enthusiasm.

At this point in the narrative, Barnabas receives one of the most lavish commendations to be found in Scripture. "He was a good man, full of the Holy Spirit and faith, and a great number of people were brought to the Lord" (11:24). These few words are a beautiful tribute to the character and effectiveness of the man known as The Encourager.

The next words of Acts raise questions: "Then Barnabas went to Tarsus to look for Saul, and when he found him, he brought him to Antioch. So for a whole year Barnabas and Saul met with the church and taught great numbers of people." Why had Saul gone home? Was he unable to preach because he had not been accepted? Had he become discouraged and given up? Whatever Saul's reason for being in Tarsus, Barnabas believed he should be in Antioch; there they worked together for a year, during which time Saul must have learned much from his friend Barnabas.

At the end of Acts 11 Barnabas and Saul appear again. The problem this time was a famine in Judea, and the church in Antioch began collecting funds to help. When the time came to find an upbeat, trustworthy person to send to Judea with the gift, the church chose Barnabas, along with his protege, Saul. Just as the church in Jerusalem had looked to The Encourager to examine the thriving church in Antioch, so now the church in Antioch sent The Encourager back to Jerusalem with a gift of hope and fellowship.

Passing the Baton

The mission trip of Acts 12 and 14 begins with the words:

While they were worshiping the Lord and fasting, the Holy Spirit said, "Set apart for me Barnabas and Saul for the work to which I have called them." So after they had fasted and prayed, they placed their hands on them and sent them off (13:2-3).

First stop on the tour was the island home of Barnabas, Cyprus. Though Saul did much of the speaking, Barnabas seems to have been perceived as the one making the key decisions. The proconsul in Cyprus sent for "Barnabas and Saul" when he wanted to hear the word of God (13:7). When the crowd in Lystra misunderstood who the men were and thought them to be gods, they gave Barnabas the name Zeus, the supreme god of the Greek pantheon, while Saul — now known as Paul — they called Hermes, the herald and messenger of the gods (14:12). After the tour, a controversy arose about the legitimacy of their mission to the Greeks. As the Jerusalem Conference proceeded, at the appropriate time "Barnabas and Paul" told the assembly about all God had done among them, and the opposition was silenced (15:12).

While Barnabas was still seen as the leader, it is clear through these chapters that Paul was coming into his own, becoming increasingly effective in his role as proclaimer and apostle to the Gentiles. Like a parent or a mentor who knows the younger has come to a position of maturity himself, Barnabas began to walk in the shadow of Paul.

His years of support and encouragement were now seeing their fulfillment as Paul began to move more toward the center of the stage — the goal toward which Barnabas had been working for years.

The last mention of Barnabas in Acts shows him, true to form, encouraging another young man. John Mark had left the first tour at midpoint for reasons not stated in the text but apparently not satisfactory to Paul. When plans for a second tour began, Barnabas wanted to take John Mark along, but Paul was skeptical. Their disagreement was sharp, and the two finally decided to part company.

From a careful reading of the text, the separation seems to have come because Barnabas was extending the same spirit of forgiveness and trust toward John Mark that he had extended to the young convert Saul years before. He was willing to give John Mark the benefit of the doubt, to give him a second chance. From the first mention of Barnabas in Acts to the last, he is consistent and unchanged, forever The Encourager. First with Saul, then with John Mark, Barnabas never seemed to grow weary of going out of his way for the benefit of others.

The Spirit of Jesus

The Encourager understood the spirit of Jesus: "For even the Son of Man did not come to be served, but to serve" (Mark 10:45). Encouraging and serving both have a common source: the willingness to deny self, while at the same time to work for the good of another.

For Jesus, the giving of Himself as a ransom for many was His ultimate proof of love; for Barnabas, the giving of himself as a supporter and defender of Christian brothers was his way of striving for the same goal. In both the vignettes recorded in Acts, the easy way out for Barnabas would have been for him to agree, "Blacklist Saul!" "Reject John Mark!" Had he done so, he could not have been faulted in either case. "Just look at their track records!" he could have said to justify his decision. But in both cases he chose to believe, he saw what they could be, he gave them his trust, and he let others know where he stood by giving open and visible support.

Today's church could use a few more people like Barnabas. If more took on the spirit of Barnabas, there would be less talk and more action. People would be building each other up, working for each other, giving courage and hope to the discouraged. Brother would be supporting brother, sister would be helping sister, and Christians would become known for their selfless devotion to strengthening and edifying one another.

If more took on the spirit of Barnabas, there would be less suspicion and more affirmation. When Brother A speaks sharply to Brother B, Brother B has a decision: Whether to write off Brother A as a crank and a grouch, or to begin showing extra compassion toward him in order to tear down the wall of hostility with additional love.

If more took on the spirit of Barnabas, there would be less criticism and more hope. When one disappoints his Christian family, will they respond, "I knew he was a phony all the time!" or, "He's come so far and grown so much — what can we do to get him back on track?" Criticism is cheap; hope is expensive, because it not only costs time, effort, and energy, it also requires risking our own good name and reputation.

A Decision of Faith

The decision to become one who serves, with Jesus, to become one who encourages, with Barnabas, is a decision that is not made lightly. The one who serves and encourages must be willing to invest the time to know people. Barnabas could not have been encouraging to Saul if he had not taken the time to come to know Saul. Barnabas could not have been encouraging to the church in Antioch if he had not taken the time to travel there and see for himself. He could not have been encouraging to John Mark if he had not come to know John Mark. Taking the time to seek people out and to become acquainted in-depth is no small commitment.

The decision to become serving, encouraging people is a decision that requires seeing people from God's standpoint, not from the human standpoint. Only with the eye of faith, hope, and love can the Christian strive to recognize potential and look beyond the external to see the soul in need as God knows it. These are perceptions that require years of living and training in the spirit of Jesus.

Beyond that, the decision to become people who serve and encourage others is a decision that requires the willingness to take risks for people. The risk may come in the form of time, emotional involvement, social acceptance, or political safety, but a risk is inherent in the role of giving oneself to other people.

Jesus who serves, Barnabas who encourages — are they not the prototype for the life of every Christian?

16

Profile of a Christian

DAN ANDERS

"The disciples were first called Christians at Antioch." Acts 11:26

We butcher many words in our everyday speech. Take the word "cool," for instance. It means "moderate in temperature" in the mouth of a meteorologist. On a teen's tongue, it will likely mean something entirely different!

Some good words get mangled in this way. "Love" is so loosely used that we probably should declare a moratorium on it. When you can "love" an Oscar Mayer wiener and God in the same breath, you have to wonder what the word does mean.

"Christian" is one of those misused words. It is so bandied about that it can mean almost anything, or nearly nothing. Just take an informal survey of your acquaintances. Ask several people "What is a Christian?" You may be surprised at the wide range of answers. "A Christian is someone who practices the Ten Commandments." Or "anyone who lives by the Golden Rule." Or "whoever believes in Jesus Christ."

My real concern is not human definitions of what a Christian is. It is much more important to know God's definition. It seems to me that this paragraph in Acts 11:19-30 is a fairly crucial one. These disciples at Syrian Antioch were the first people to be called Christians. I believe that this section of Scripture shows us some real benchmarks to help us define what a Christian is.

A Christian Has Heard about Jesus

The paragraph begins with a basic truth. Disciples from Cyprus and Cyrene came to Antioch as a spin-off from the Jerusalem pogrom against the church. These persecuted preachers were "telling them the good news about the Lord Jesus" (Acts 11:20).

That's pretty basic, isn't it? A Christian has heard the gospel of Jesus Christ. You can't get more fundamental than that. A Christian knows who Jesus is and what He did, as that good news was proclaimed by the early spokesmen of the gospel.

I encourage you to do a little Bible study on your own. It will only take a short while, and it will pay big dividends. Take an unmarked New Testament. Read those first gospel sermons. You can find summaries of them preserved by Luke in Acts 2:22ff.; 3:12ff.; 4:8ff.; 7:1ff.; 10:34ff.; and 13:16ff. Compile a list of the main points in these sermons. I think you will discover that "the gospel" is a simple proclamation of Jesus' saving ministry in and for the world.

Surely it was this same message that the traveling evangelists preached in Antioch. It always takes this message to make a person a Christian.

In his Yale lectures, George A. Buttrick hit close to the heart of the gospel.

> It is a faithful saying and worthy of all acceptation that apostolic preaching had but one word — Christ, from whom all other words derived their life. The night of pagan cults had a thousand stars; the day of the apostles' gospel but one Sun. He was Alpha and Omega. There was no other name in earth or heaven. All their arguments were clinched, and all their commands were sealed in Him.

Without the good news of Jesus, there can be no Christians.

Christians Are International

Up until this time, the gospel had been preached only to Jews. To be sure, the Samaritans converted in Acts 8 were a mixed race. But they still had Jewish blood. The household of Cornelius were the first Gentiles who heard the good news of Jesus and became His followers (see Acts

10, 11). Now the gulf that yawned between Jews and Gentiles is bridged in the first predominantly Gentile congregation at Antioch.

From the start, it had been God's purpose that all humanity should be reached by the good news of salvation in Christ. Jesus' final charge to His apostles had commissioned them to "make disciples of all nations" (Matthew 28:19). On the Day of Pentecost, Peter had quoted Joel's ancient prophecy that God would pour out His Spirit "on all people" (Acts 2:17). He preached that the promise of divine forgiveness and Spirit-given life was "for all who are far off — for all whom the Lord our God will call" (Acts 2:39).

But it had taken the church about fifteen years to catch up with its own gospel! They may have proclaimed that the message was for all. However, it took a savage persecution and the further revelation of God to push them to share the gospel with all.

This universal gospel, first practiced in the church at Antioch, is captured in John Oxenham's lovely hymn.

> In Christ there is no east or west,
> In Him no south or north;
> But one great fellowship of love
> Throughout the whole wide earth.
>
> Join hands, then, brothers of the faith,
> Whate'er your race may be.
> Who serves my Father as a son
> Is surely kin to me.

Christians belong to no one nation or race, no one culture or class. Every person of every tribe and tongue may wear Christ's name.

A Christian Responds to Jesus

Luke clearly understood that being a Christian meant more than hearing the gospel. When those early missionaries preached, "the Lord's hand was with them, and a great number of people believed and turned to the Lord" (Acts 11:21). The gospel demands response. Every person who hears it must decide what he will do with the claims and call of Jesus.

When the gospel is preached and heard, some people will believe the message and trust Jesus Christ as Savior and Lord. Obviously, not all who hear will believe. Some will resist the message. Because of family ties, or personal pride, or the influence of friends, some will always hear without faith. As in Jesus' story of the different soils, some hearers still reject the gospel message and its demands (see Matthew 13:1-9, 18-23).

Thank God, there will always be some who hear and believe! Paul's statement has proven true uncounted times — "So faith comes from what is heard, and what is heard comes by the preaching of Christ" (Romans 10:17).

At this point, Luke's narrative makes a subtle but significant distinction. The translation of the New International Version is a little misleading: "a great number of people believed and turned to the Lord." The Revised Standard Version is closer to Luke's original words: "a great number that believed turned to the Lord." That small difference is important.

Luke's words clearly mean that there were people who believed in Christ, but never turned to Him. "A great number that believed turned," but not all that believed turned. You can believe in Jesus without turning to Him.

I know that this is true because I have seen it happen. I have known people convinced that they ought to follow Jesus. They believed the message. They even were willing to say that Jesus is Lord. But that is as far as it went! They would not submit their lives to Christ.

I know that a person can believe without turning because it happened in Bible times. These dire words are recorded in John 12:42, 43. "Yet at the same time many even among the leaders believed in Him. But because of the Pharisees they would not confess their faith for fear they would be put out of the synagogue; for they loved praise from men more than praise from God." These people believed in Christ, but would not turn to Him.

It is not enough to trust Jesus in your heart. That does not make one a Christian! You must turn to Christ to become a Christian. How, then, does one turn to Christ? Luke's history shows us. You can find it over and over in the Book of Acts, but two verses adequately illustrate the point.

The gospel was taken to Samaria by Philip following the persecution after Stephen's murder (Acts 8:1-5). "But when they believed Philip as he preached the good news of the kingdom of God and the name of Jesus Christ, they were baptized, both men and women" (Acts 8:12).

The same thing is repeated years later and hundreds of miles away in Paul's mission at Corinth. "Crispus, the synagogue ruler, and his entire household believed in the Lord; and many of the Corinthians who heard him believed and were baptized" (Acts 18:8).

Isn't that plain? People heard the gospel. They believed in Jesus. They were baptized. They had turned to the Lord. Many Bible scholars grasp this pattern of truth. Dietrich Bonhoeffer, who was martyred by the Nazis in the closing days of World War II, expressed it like this:

> When He called men to Him, Jesus was summoning them to a *visible act of obedience*. To follow Jesus was a public act. Baptism is similarly a public event, for it is the means whereby a member is grafted on to the visible body of Christ (Galatians 3:26f.; 1 Corinthians 12:13).

According to the New Testament Scriptures, a Christian was one who believed in Christ and turned to Him in baptism.

A Christian Grows in Christ

Belief and baptism are just the beginning of a Christian's new life. Barnabas was sent to Antioch by the apostles in Jerusalem to help the fledgling congregation develop spiritually. "He encouraged them all to remain true to the Lord with all their hearts" (Acts 11:24). Later, with the help of Saul of Tarsus, he "met with the church and taught great numbers of people." This crash course in Christianity went on for a whole year (Acts 11:26).

There have always been people who began greatly and finished poorly. As a dieter, I have lost hundreds of pounds. The only trouble is it's always the same ones — the first four or five! It doesn't accomplish much to diet, or study French, or take up jogging, or become a Christian — unless you stay at it. It takes perseverance to succeed at anything.

In 1834 Richard Wagner wrote his first opera, "The Wedding." His teacher snubbed it as "atrocious." In 1835 he composed "The Fairies." He couldn't find a producer. His work, "Ban on Love," opened and closed the same night! He was discouraged and broke, but he wouldn't quit. Finally one of his operas became a hit. Today his monumental music dramas are performed regularly around the world.

A Christian doesn't retire on the far side of the baptistry. He learns and grows in Christ.

A Christian Is Generous

Sometime during that year of instruction, prophets from Jerusalem visited the Antioch congregation. One of them predicted that a severe famine would strike the whole Roman empire. The Antioch church probably had already heard about the financial distress of the Jerusalem church (Acts 4:32-35; 6:1). They immediately realized that successive crop failures would multiply Judean problems. So "the disciples, each according to his ability, decided to provide help for the brothers living in Judea. This they did, sending their gift to the elders by Barnabas and Saul" (Acts 11:29).

As far as I have been able to determine, this was the first case of international relief in history! We take such global concern for granted today. When an earthquake hits Mexico, or a famine strikes Ethiopia, our first instinct is to help. That has not always been the case. In the ancient world, a foreigner was always the enemy. For Syrians to want to help Jews was unheard of — then and now!

But there it is: "The disciples each" — a personal choice — "according to his ability" — an individual response — provided help. A Christian is a generous person.

In his *Diary of a Country Priest*, George Bernanos tells a moving story. A doctor informs a priest that he is dying of stomach cancer. The priest, at first bewildered, says a prayer.

> Dear God, I give You all willingly. But I don't know how to give, I just let them take. The best is to remain quiet. Because though I may not know how to give, You know how to take . . . Yet I would have wished to be, once, just once, magnificently generous to You.

That's about it, isn't it? If we are really Christians, we keep trying somehow, just once, to be "magnificently generous" in what we do for God. That is what it means to be a Christian.

17

United with Christ

JOHN GIPSON

It's to a new life that God is calling us. Not to some new steps in life, some new motives, ways, or prospects, but to a new life. Every Christian can rejoice in hearing the apostle Paul say, "Therefore, if any one is in Christ, he is a new creation; the old has passed away, behold, the new has come" (2 Corinthians 5:17). In Christ one enters "the land of beginning again."

To be a Christian means the identification of the individual with Christ. It is not merely believing a scheme of doctrine, but an absolute union with Christ in spiritual experience. Someone has pointed out that "nothing seems to be more characteristic of the apostle Paul than the way in which, in almost every epistle, he describes the Christian life as going step-by-step with the life of Christ from earthly humiliation and death to heavenly triumph." And this is clearly seen in the words he addresses to the Colossians. "For you have died, and your life is hid with Christ in God. When Christ who is our life appears, then you also will appear with Him in glory" (Colossians 3:3, 4). In this short reading we see (1) our death with Christ, (2) our life with Christ, and (3) our destiny with Christ.

Our Death with Christ

Nothing could speak more eloquently of the love Christ has for us than to see his nail-pierced form hanging on the cross for our sins. "Greater love has no man than this, that a man lay down his life for his friends" (John 15:13).

Every such act of love impresses us. From the fourth century B.C. comes the story of Damon and Pythias. Pythias was condemned to death for plotting against Dionysius of Syracuse. Desiring time to arrange his affairs before his execution, Damon placed himself in the hands of Dionysius as a substitute for Pythias and was willing to die if Pythias failed to return. In fact, Damon prayed the gods to delay the return of Pythias till after his own execution in his stead. The fatal day arrived. Dionysius sat on a moving throne drawn by six white horses. Damon mounted the scaffold and calmly addressed the spectators:

> My prayer is heard; the gods are propitious, for the winds have been contrary till yesterday. Pythias could not come; he could not conquer impossibilities; he will be here tomorrow, and the blood which is shed today shall have ransomed the life of my friend. Oh! Could I erase from your bosoms every mean suspicion of the honour of Pythias, I should go to my death as I would to my bridal. My friend will be found noble, his truth unimpeachable; he will speedily prove it; he is now on his way, accusing himself, the adverse elements, and the gods; but I haste to prevent his speed. Executioner, do your office.

As he closed, a voice in the distance cried, "Stop the execution!" which was repeated by the whole assembly. A man rode up crying, "You are safe, my beloved friend." Damon replied, "Fatal haste, cruel impatience! Since I cannot die to save you, I will not survive you."

When the king heard these words he was moved to tears. Ascending the scaffold, he cried, "Live, live, ye incomparable pair!"

Such a demonstration of love is moving to all of us. But the story of Damon and Pythias, as beautiful as it is, pales when placed side by side with Christ's matchless love. One essential difference lies in the fact that Christ died for us when we were enemies, not friends. How could one behold the cross of Christ and not be lost in "wonder, love and praise"?

But if I am to be united with Christ, His crucifixion must have its counterpart in me. "For you have died," said the apostle Paul in Colossians 3:3. And this death is with Christ (Colossians 2:20). When did it happen? At the time of my obedience to the gospel. "Do you not know that all of us who have been baptized into Christ Jesus were baptized into His death? We were buried therefore with Him by baptism into death, so that as Christ was raised from the dead by the glory of the Father, we too might walk in newness of life" (Romans 6:3, 4).

Because Paul had been baptized into the death of Christ he could say, "I have been crucified with Christ; it is no longer I who live, but Christ who lives in me; and the life I now life in the flesh I live by faith in the Son of God who loved me and gave himself for me" (Galatians 2:20).

In these words we have depicted the surrendered life in a nutshell. It is nothing less than crucifixion with Christ. Unfortunately, the trouble with too much religion today is that it is nothing more than a spiritual cosmetic, adding a touch of color to a countenance not radically changed.

If we have really been crucified with Christ, then at least three important things have happened:

There has been a death to sin. Such a separation is not easy, but it is necessary. "So you also must consider yourselves dead to sin and alive to God in Christ Jesus" (Romans 6:11). "How can we who died to sin still live in it?" (Romans 6:2). As painful and difficult as dying to sin is, it can be accomplished by the Spirit (Romans 8:13). Ambrose Bierce once looked at the so-called Christians around him and said, "A Christian is one who follows the teachings of Christ insofar as they are not inconsistent with a life of sin." Ouch! If that is true, it shouldn't be. Once as sinners we were dead in sin. Now as believers we are dead to sin.

> Buried with Christ, my blessed Redeemer,
> Dead to the old life of folly and sin;
> Satan may call, the world may entreat me,
> There is no voice that answers within.
> T. O. Chisholm

There has been a death to self. "I am crucified," said the apostle Paul. He had met the requirement of Christ who said, "If any man would come after me, let him deny himself and take up his cross and follow me" (Matthew 16:24). In fact, someone has described the cross as the letter "I" crossed out. This death to self is the very reason Christianity can never be popular. Not many are really willing to say:

Take my life, and let it be
Consecrated, Lord, to Thee.

There has been a death to the world. The Christian is one who has cut loose from "things on earth." As the apostle said, "The world has been crucified to me, and I to the world" (Galatians 6:14). He had a first-class funeral for the present age and all those things which belong to it. And that should be true of every child of God. Our feet might be on the earth, but our heads should be in heaven. When we become dead to the world, all of those earthly pleasures, treasures, honors, and values that tend to draw our souls away from Christ lose their charm. As Paul said, "But whatever gain I had, I counted as loss for the sake of Christ. Indeed I count everything as loss because of the surpassing worth of knowing Christ Jesus my Lord. For His sake I have suffered the loss of all things, and count them as refuse, in order that I may gain Christ" (Philippians 3:7, 8).

Our Life with Christ

The Christian who is dead and buried to sin, self, and the world is nevertheless alive. "Your life is hid with Christ in God." What a blessing! There is double security for it is with Christ and it is in God. As Roy Laurin has said, "No wonder Chrysostom could answer his emperor so confidently. The monarch threatened to take Chrysostom's life unless he recanted his faith and renounced Christ. 'You cannot, your majesty' was the saint's confident reply, 'For my life is hid with Christ in God.' It is conceivable that the King could have destroyed Chrysostom's body but in so doing he could not reach Chrysostom's life for that was in the double security of being 'with Christ in God.' "

Rejoice, believer in the Lord,
Who makes your cause His own;
The hope that's founded on His word
Can ne'er be overthrown.
Though many foes beset your road,
And feeble is your arm,
Your life is hid with Christ in God,
Beyond the reach of harm.
John Newton

Christ is the source of our life. When Jesus announced His mission to men He said, "I came that they may have life, and have it abundantly" (John 10:10). He intended to smite death with life, and has done so for every child of God. We were dead in trespasses and sins, but life has been given (Ephesians 2:1). "And this is the testimony, that God gave us eternal life, and this life is in His Son. He who has the Son has life; he who has not the Son of God has not life" (I John 5:11, 12). Rejoice! We have in us another life, derived from Jesus.

Christ is the object of our life. To the Christian Jesus Christ is not only the most important thing in life; He is life itself. Paul calls Christ "our life" (Colossians 3:4). And he says, "For me to live is Christ" (Philippians 1:21). In the words of William Barclay, "This is the kind of peak of devotion which we can only dimly understand and which we can only haltingly and imperfectly express. Sometimes we say of a man, 'Music is his life — sport is his life — he lives for his work.' Such a man finds life and all that life means in music, in sport, in work, as the case may be. For the Christian, Christ is his life. Jesus Christ dominates his thought and fills his life."

Can you imagine what would happen in our world if every Christian could truly say, "For me to live is Christ?" Someone has suggested, "The chief reason why Christianity does not yet pervade the world is that Christ does not pervade the life of Christians." We become standardized without being Christianized. We hold a form of doctrine, but deny its power. We are content to march in the "Parade of the Wooden Soldiers" without putting on Christ and living him day by day.

Our life must be so "hid with Christ in God" that it is "like the spring of that mystical river of the water of life which flows forth from the throne of God and of the Lamb."

My life I bring to Thee;
I would not be my own;
O Savior, let me be Thine ever,
Thine alone.
    Frances R. Havergal

Christ is the example of our life. "For to this you have been called, because Christ also suffered for you, leaving you an example, that you should follow in His steps" (I Peter 1:21). In 1896, Charles M. Sheldon wrote a book entitled *In His Steps*. He explored what would take place in any town or city if every church member should begin to do as Jesus would do. It is not easy to go into details of the result. But I urge you to read the book and see how many changes would be made. Certain things would be impossible that are now practiced by church members, and other works, often neglected, would come to the fore. If we would leave our nominal Christianity behind and follow Jesus we would turn the world upside down. Are we ready to imitate Jesus? To do as He would do? To walk in His steps?

Our Destiny with Christ

If we have experienced death and life with Christ, then our destiny is glorious. "When Christ who is our life appears, then you also will appear with Him in glory" (Colossians 3:4). Notice that there is no "if" concerning Christ's appearing. Inspiration uses the positive word "when." While He was upon earth Christ pledged Himself, both to His friends and to His foes, to return. And the Christian lives in expectation of His coming. As Paul told the Thessalonians, "You turned to God from idols, to serve a living and true God, and to wait for His Son from heaven, whom He raised from the dead, Jesus who delivers us from the wrath to come" (I Thessalonians 1:9, 10).

The goal and destiny of the Christian is not a grave in a cemetery or a crypt in a mausoleum. It is the future glory of the Son of God. This Jesus who once appeared in weakness and humiliation is coming back in power and majesty and glory and "then shall ye also appear with Him in glory."

"Beloved, we are God's children now; it does not yet appear what we shall be, but we know that when He appears we shall be like Him, for we shall see Him as He is" (I John 3:2). One noted author has said that it may well be that the best illumination of this passage is the Scottish paraphrase of it:

> Behold the amazing gift of love
> the Father hath bestow'd
> On us, the sinful sons of men,
> to call us sons of God!
> Concealed as yet this honour lies,
> by this dark world unknown,
> A world that knew not when He came,
> even God's eternal Son.

High is the rank we now possess,
but higher we shall rise;
Though what we shall hereafter be
is hid from mortal eyes.
Our souls, we know, when He appears,
shall bear His image bright;
For all his glory, full disclosed,
shall open to our sight.
A hope so great, and so divine,
may trials well endure;
And purge the soul from sense and sin,
as Christ Himself is pure.

To be a child of God now is wonderful. It is a sharing of the death and life of Christ. But to contemplate the future is glorious beyond compare. To see Christ, to be like Christ, to appear with Him in glory is a destiny which could only be conceived and accomplished by God. Praise His name!

18

All Things Are Yours!

GEOFFREY ELLIS

Come, let us do a little boasting together, and let us boast in the Lord.

However we may want to capture it — "We're number one!" "We've got it made!" "We're on the winning team!" — literally, in Christ, we have achieved the ultimate. Victory is ours. We have overcome!

The superlative joys of Christ were consciously present in the apostle Paul: often in the midst of basic teaching he would rocket out of the human condition to capture the orbiting "spiritual blessings in heavenly realms" that are in Christ. Such was the case in the early portions of his first letter to the Corinthians. While Paul was working over the problems of human wisdom and the divisiveness of the party spirit, it came to him what can set men free from narrow thinking:

> So then, no more boasting about men! All things are
> yours, whether Paul or Apollos or Cephas or the world
> or life or death or the present or the future—all are
> yours, and you are of Christ, and Christ is from God
> (I Corinthians 3:21-23 NIV).

Having entered upon the privileges of God, it is beneath the Christian to conduct himself as a worldling, impoverished in understanding, conduct, and values. The rich opportunity before Christians everywhere is to possess our possessions, to enter into the true nobility that befits children of God, and to put off those "weak and beggardly" elements that mark the world.

"No More Boasting About Men"

One of the messages most urgently needed by North Americans today is given in this restraint by Paul: "So then, no more boasting about men." Our politics are captured by the personality cult. Our children's heroes are the entertainers. Our infatuation with "leadership" has left us easy prey for the manipulators. The modern god of the masses, humanism's super man, has led us to the final idolatry (Romans 1:23). The most unseemly slavery of all occurs when we voluntarily prostrate ourselves before the imagined greatness of others.

Today's excess goes beyond esteeming a person for his work's sake (I Thessalonians 5:13), or honoring one where honor is due (Romans 13:7). Today's infatuation with the great among us is more than the humble submitting "one to another" (Ephesians 5:21). The current "standing ovation" syndrome reflects a hunger for human glory. We stand up and shout, "All right!" with our clenched fists thrust skyward when our hero crosses the goal; somehow we are part of that action and can bask in the victory light so precious "to the fans."

Our proneness to exalt unduly our fellow man is sadly evident in the church today, even as it was in Paul's day. Divisions within the brotherhood have occurred in recent times when men with a high self-regard have sought and received the support of followers afflicted with the party spirit. Both leaders and followers share responsibility for division. It was the follower that Paul condemned when he reminded the Corinthians, "One of you says, 'I follow Paul'; still another, 'I follow Apollos'; another, 'I follow Cephas'; still another, 'I follow Christ' " (I Corinthians 1:12). Without those willing to boast in men, the party leaders would be kings without kingdoms.

Our century has seen elders functioning as monarchs and evangelists acting as rulers. Without the complicity of brethren ready to elevate men unduly, these departures from the New Testament pattern would not be possible. Not the kingship of Christ, but His role as the Good Shepherd is the elder's model for leadership (I Peter 5:2-4). The authority of the evangelist is contained in the Word he preaches rather than in the office he holds; it is found in the moral force of his personal example (I Timothy 4:12). The guiding principle that regulates leaders and followers in the church is ". . . and you are all brothers" (Matthew 23:8). We have only one Lord in the church, Jesus Christ (Ephesians 4:5). Our leaders' sole function is to assist Christians that they might "in all things grow up into Him who is the Head, that is Christ" (Ephesians 4:15).

Is it possible that our readiness to boast in men grows out of a frustrated desire to boast in ourselves? Recently, a psychologist of the University of Alberta advocated group bragging sessions. Participants were encouraged "to announce their strengths" to each other. Bragging how good they were, they were directed to a large box where they could throw the bushels they had used to hide their own candles! This assertiveness training is characteristic of the spirit of our time. Paul spoke to this spirit when he echoed the word of God given through Jeremiah the prophet:

> Let not the wise man boast of his wisdom,
> or the strong man boast of his strength
> or the rich man boast of his riches,
> but let him who boasts boast about this:
> that he understands and knows me,
> that I am the Lord, who exercises kindness,
> justice and righteousness on earth,
> for in these I delight (Jeremiah 9:23, 24).

"So then, no more boasting about men . . ." rather, "let him who boasts boast in the Lord" (I Corinthians 3:21; 1:31).

"All Things Are Yours"

The Corinthian Christians addressed by Paul were notorious for their pride in their human wisdom, for their blase spirituality — yes, their carnality — even their ignorance of basic Christian truths. Yet, Paul saluted them as "the church of God in Corinth" and affirmed this magnificent privilege: "All things are yours." Clearly, here is the ultimate statement regarding the graciousness of God to His redeemed. This is in keeping with the plan of God to adopt His creatures as His children: "How great is the love the Father has lavished on us that we should be called the children of God! And this is what we are!" (I John 3:1). "The Spirit Himself testifies with our spirit that we are God's children. Now if we are children, then we are heirs — heirs of God and co-heirs with Christ . . ." (Romans 8:16, 17a). If, because we are God's children, all things are ours, how important is it for us to have an accurate inventory of our blessings, be grateful for them, and live joyfully in them.

Included in the "all things" of our possessions are:

The greatest men of every age: Paul, Peter, and Apollos were great sources of strength, direction, and example for the Corinthian church, indeed for the church of the first century and of every age. But Paul asked concerning himself and Apollos, "What, after all, are we?" His answer: "Only servants, through whom you came to believe" (I Corinthians 3:5). Christ's church was not to be just another human structure in which the power of the few controlled the many. "Whoever wants to become great among you must be your servant, and whoever wants to be first must be your slave" (Matthew 20:26, 27).

Christ truly encourages the realization of every good within the capabilities and circumstances of each person. Christianity is the original "human potential" movement. But quite simply we are to acknowledge that God is the first cause of every human accomplishment. We can respect the high achievers among us, be inspired by their example, and be heartened by their courage; in this way we possess them. Yet, only God is worthy of our devotion.

The world in which we live: The preacher C. R. Nichols, short in stature, dignified in mien, was accosted by a women in a store one day: "You walk like you own the world!" His reply, "My father does." Christians have an objective view of the world. They understand that lifeless (inorganic) matter is not eternal. They understand that its myriad life-forms are purposefully designed and created, not the result of the blind gropings of some chance life-force (evolution). Every bush is ablaze with the glory of God. Only God can make a tree! In the early stages of modern scientific development, the men who had the confidence that the world was ordered, predictable, and under "laws" of nature, were men who lived in the Christian tradition. Our God is not "the God of the gaps — that is a temporary superstition covering the things we cannot yet explain. Rather, He is the God of the cosmos: every day He is appearing more powerful, wise, and present through the unfolding knowledge of our biosphere and the broader universe, His handiwork. ". . . His eternal power and divine nature — have been clearly seen, being understood from what has been made" (Romans 1:20). More than any, Christians possess the world. They know its maker. They answer His charge to "work it and take care of it" (Genesis 2:15). The world is "user friendly," marvelously adjusted for the enjoyment and support of the human family. We thank God for "the fruitful seasons" and our "daily bread." The world is ours.

Time and eternity: Life and death, the present and the future, all belong to the Christian through the gracious provision of our Father.

Christians possess the moment. They know the value of time and redeem it "for the days are evil." (Ephesians 5:16). That is, they recognize the urgency of accomplishing good during the time that is given each day as the gift from God. They are engaged in His work and are pressing to the fulfillment of His eternal purpose. They know that time is linear, not cyclical. Their days will shortly end. Christians possess the time, for they know their origin, their place and purpose, and their destiny. Christians possess the present because they are blessed by the indwelling Spirit of God to empower (Ephesians 3:16), and by God's providential care to protect. The Christian's confidence is that God is working through each event, both good and bad, to bring about good for His faithful (Romans 8:28).

As well, the future and even death are possessed by the Christian. He knows not what the future will bring, but He knows the future is controlled by a hands-on God. Our God has proven His overarching regulation of the affairs of men. The movements of history were His pallet, colors, and canvas, as He portrayed and brought into reality, "in the fullness of time," His grand design — salvation for mankind through the gift of His Son. And now the tides in the affairs of men are pressing inexorably to the climax: "And this gospel of the kingdom will be preached in the whole world as a testimony to all nations, and then the end will come" (Matthew 23:14).

For the Christian, time spills into eternity, or better still, eternity intrudes into time. Both time and eternity are possessed by the Christian: "I tell you the truth, he who believes has everlasting life" (John 6:47). That being so, death, man's fearful enemy, is for the Christian merely a transition, a passage to infinitely better things. "Dear friends, now we are the children of God, and what we will be has not yet been made known. But we know that when He appears, we shall be like Him, for we shall see Him as He is" (I John 3:2). The future is ours, eternity is ours, because the fearful consequences of a hopeless death have been removed by the triumphant resurrection of Christ, causing us to exclaim:

"Where, O death, is your victory?

Where, O death, is your sting?" (I Corinthians 15:55).

"And You Are of Christ"

All things are yours, except, that is, for one thing — yourself!
The only way to possess all things is to be wholly possessed by Jesus

Christ the Lord. This is the consistent, persistent theme of the New Testament. Jesus' supreme sacrifice secured our salvation. Likewise, it is also necessary for each of us to die to ourselves to enter into that salvation. Jesus stated emphatically, "I tell you the truth, unless a kernel of wheat falls to the ground and dies, it remains only a single seed. But if it dies, it produces many seeds. The man who loves his life will lose it, while the man who hates his life in this world will keep it for eternal life" (John 12:24, 25). This is the dimension of Christ's lordship for us. This is the meaning and the pointing of our baptism (Romans 6:5-10). This is the teaching and the reminder that comes to us at each gathering around the Lord's table. This is Paul's declaration: "And He died for all, that those who live should no longer live for themselves but for Him who died for them and was raised again" (II Corinthians 5:15). This is our understanding who, as disciples, take up our crosses daily — our cross is the symbol of our death to ourselves — for the sake of the gospel (Mark 8:34, 35). "Whether we live (life is ours) or whether we die (death is ours), we are the Lord's!" (Romans 14:8). And to acknowledge the lordship of Christ is not burdensome; it is not the path to exploitation, and abuse, and reduction. Rather, Christ came that we might have the abundant life (John 10:10). He invites an exchange of burdens, ours for His, our wearisome, unbearable burdens, for His yoke which is "easy and light" (Matthew 11:30).

"And Christ is of God"

Literally, the twenty-third verse of I Corinthians 3 reads, "you of Christ, Christ of God," meaning "belonging to." Christ is uniquely, solely, the "only-begotten" Son of God (John 1:14, 18). There are two senses in which Jesus is "of " God. First, He is God. He is God the Son, the "Word of God" (John 1:1). "The Son is the radiance of God's glory and the exact representation of His being" (Hebrews 1:3). And while He dwelt among men as a man, "in Him was the fullness of the godhead bodily" (Colossians 2:9). Secondly, as fully man on earth, Jesus was wholly in submission to God. His resignation was, ". . . nevertheless, not my will but yours be done" (Luke 22:42). "During the days of Jesus' life on earth He offered up prayers and petitions with loud cries and tears to the One who could save Him from death, and He was heard because of His reverent submission. Although He was a son, He learned obedience from what He suffered and, once made perfect, He became the source of eternal salvation for all who obey Him . . ." (Hebrews 5:7-9).

It is precisely because Christ is God's possession that Christians can believe in the truth of the superlative promise: "All things are yours!" Twice stated by Paul in our text, this overwhelming declaration of the Christian's good fortune and high favor echo Paul's all powerful exclamation:

"Praise be to the God and Father of our Lord Jesus Christ, who has blessed us in the heavenly realms with every spiritual blessing in Christ" (Ephesians 1:3).

Thanks be to God for the "incomparable riches of His grace", and "for His indescribable gift", and "for the inexpressible and glorious joy it brings!" (Ephesians 2:7; II Corinthians 9:15; I Peter 1:8).

19

Where There Is Hope, There Is Life

WILLIAM YOUNG

Some say life has no purpose. It is merely a series of accidents. It is time, plus space, plus chance. Writers, scientists, educators, and historians have added their own personal notes of human meaninglessness. French philosopher and author Voltaire (1694-1778) wrote: "Strike out a few sages and the crowd of human beings is nothing but a horrible assemblage of unfortunate criminals and the whole globe contains nothing but corpses — I wish I had never been born." The despair reflected in Voltaire could easily account for earlier predictions he made regarding the Bible. He predicted that in 100 years after his time, the Bible would be outmoded and found only in museums. One hundred years later, Voltaire's house was owned by the Geneva Bible Society, and in recent times 92 volumes of Voltaire's works were sold for two dollars.

Futility and loneliness is in dramatic contrast to the commitment of believers in God. Historian H. G. Wells (1866-1946) said: "And here I am at 65, still asking for peace. Peace is just a helpful dream, but essentially an impossible dream." A Christian believes that there is a supreme, divine God who created man and who has spoken to us revealing who we are (sinners) and who we can become (sons). The Christian believes in God and in the destiny of God's purpose for man (Romans 8:28 and 12:1-2).

In a significant speech to Greek philosophers in Athens (Acts

17:22-31), Paul contrasted the pagan worship of superstition to the commitment of worship to the one true God of heaven and earth. Paul said that man is God's creation and lives only by the sustaining power of God (vss. 25-26). We cannot declare independence or self-sufficiency because God, who made us, arranges our lives. Man is the offspring of God (vss. 28-29).

Lightheartedly, we often attribute our lives and welfare to "good luck," "fortune," or "mother nature." These are foolish claims to independence. We don't realize our true potential, nor do we understand the forces at work in our lives. We are like the caterpillar who watched the butterfly darting about and remarked, "You'll never get me up in one of those things." A caterpillar may be ignorant of its connection with a butterfly, which doesn't present a moral crisis, but man is facing a serious dilemma when he fails to understand the purpose for which he was created. Without conscious and reverent awareness of God, we will all look at life with very little hope of fulfilling achievement and connecting purpose.

Regardless of how primitive or sophisticated the Athenians perceived themselves to be, Paul respectfully approached the Greeks about their idolatrous worship. He felt, as did Jeremiah (10:5-11), that such worship and trust in carved idols was unintelligent. Jeremiah describes idols as a "scarecrow in a melon patch . . . they must be carried because they cannot walk" (vs. 6). He also says that those who carved the idols out of wood or stone were more clever than their sculptured creations (vss. 8-11). Perhaps we see our age as being more developed, beyond worshipping carved trees, but we show similar tendencies to live for intelligence, success, or pleasure. Whatever is most important to us in life becomes our object of worship or devotion. Call it what we will, this is a form of idol worship (Matthew 6:21).

The Bible calls covetousness "idolatry" (Colossians 3:5), which is grasping concern for wealth or possessions in lavish devotion for ourselves. Commitment is dependence. Whatever we give our lives to seek out, have, or control, we depend on it for our satisfaction. All dependence is a necessary reliance on (or slavery to) something or someone superior to ourselves, without which we are unable to enjoy life. What a pity if, consciously or unconsciously, our priority commitment is to the temporary, unfeeling, mindless things of earthly ambitions. Wealth, power, prestige — what do they care about the real person? Money or fame use us — they don't care for us.

God cares and He has done everything to reveal this care. He made us and our world of animate and inanimate creations. He grieves over our rebellious, sinful disregard for His guiding will. He sent His only son to pay the death penalty for our sin in order to win us back to His will and purpose for us.

When we live only for ourselves, we are the loneliest creatures on earth. The greatest evidence of loneliness today is the number of people who express a complete lack of purpose in life — an emptiness, a basic lack of meaning for human existence. We know that loneliness is caused by broken or imperfect relationships with others; therefore, we struggle against it by attaching ourselves to group associations, families, labor guilds, civic, fraternal, professional organizations, and even religious groups. Regardless of how we may be surrounded with people or things, unless we discover a uniting fellowship with God we will be isolated, alone, and uncommitted to the only real purpose for our creation in God's image (John 5:40; 6:45, 48, 53).

Paul urged the Christians in Rome to commit themselves to God as "living, holy sacrifices." The slaughtering of animals for sacrifices to God has long since ceased. People, alive with Christ in themselves, are to offer their devotion to God as holy persons transformed into the image of His Son (Romans 12:1-2; 8:29). Unless we make the difficult decision to reject worldly, inferior definitions of life, we will fail to resemble the model man, Christ (Acts 20:24; James 4:14).

It is practical to protect many aspects of our lives by purchasing insurance —life, accident, health, theft, property, warranty, job, retirement, disability, and death. This is often done at considerable sacrifice because we believe insurance policies are sensible precautions against unexpected and undesired incidents. But man is more than a body housing intelligence! There is something more to life than merely clothing, feeding, sheltering, and educating ourselves until we die. We can become too preoccupied with building 70 or more years of existence and neglect God's call to holiness.

Like Israel of old who labored for a fall harvest which never seemed good enough; ate and drank but were never filled; were clothed but never warmed; and earned wages only to put them in purses that were full of holes (Haggai 1:6), we busy ourselves with survival while holy purposes lie unattended.

Paul reasoned with Christians in Rome to perceive believers as freed from the death sentence of sin, to be gratefully offering living and holy devotion to God who freed them. Would spiritually maturing and grateful children of God want to conform to a world indifferent to godly respect and holy service? Believers are no longer condemned and do not continue wearing handcuffs. Those who are cleared of the guilt of sin do not remain enslaved to the old nature. When given new garments, we do not prefer rags. We have been given the water of life to carry, but not in a leaky bucket!

Our new self or nature is bought with a great price (I Corinthians 6:15, 10), and because we are His, everything else in life is dedicated to the glory and honor of the Lord (I Corinthians 7:29-31). Christians are committed to a higher life. We offer ourselves in obedient thanksgiving to God (Hebrews 13:14-16). Our holiness is really God's holiness flowing through our submitted lives.

Surrendered lifestyles are empowered by God's holy presence and have a purpose for living which influences others. "I would give anything to believe — anything! I envy my friends who do." Do you know someone like that — someone who wants faith but feels in today's world that it is not possible? What can any person do to endure world conditions impacted by growing disbelief? We need people who will prove God, not by argument, but by experience and example (Psalms 34:8 and I Peter 2:3).

Changed (transformed) lives are indisputable proof of faithful convictions. God is proved when believers demonstrate the committed work of His will in obedient lives. This is what Jesus told Philip (John 14:8-11). A changed life doesn't come about primarily because one has accepted a set of ideas, but because one has committed himself to the person of Christ whose teaching is superior when it is practiced. Believers trust in Christ to make the changes needed, first in ourselves and then in the world we are called to influence (John 6:67-68).

"Ideas," says George Eliot, "are poor ghosts until they become incarnate in a person." Christ is the one perfect combination of words and deeds. With Him as our center, we can make progress with His truth and avert the traps of saying but not being! (Matthew 23:1-7). Christ urges us to see how great will be the darkness of our lives if what we proclaim as light isn't evident in our own lives (Matthew 6:23; 5:14-16).

About the early disciples of the Lord, Albert Schweitzer once remarked, "They were drawn to Him before they knew who He was." Perhaps the whirlpool of human disbelief in God could be stilled by persons drawn to God and alive with His Spirit.

The teachings of Christ are full of promise, not nostalgia. Not things as they used to be — but as they will be (Mark 1:15). We often say, "Where there is life, there is hope." Because of Christ it is even better to believe that where there is hope there is life (I Corinthians 15:19; Romans 24, 25).

20

Preaching as Counseling

PAUL FAULKNER

> Among all my patients in the second half of life — that is to say, over thirty-five, there has not been one whose problem in the last resort was not that of finding a religious outlook on life. It is safe to say that everyone of them fell ill because he had lost that which the living religions of every age have given to their followers, and none of them has been really healed who did not regain his religious outlook.
>
> Carl Gustav Jung, *Modern Man in Search of a Soul*

Historically, the priest and the healer have a common ancestor in the ancient priest (Leviticus 13). Even until recent times, the priest and the healer were one person. Then the healers — psychiatrists, social workers, psychologists, marriage/family therapists, and other specialists — began practicing apart from the church — for fees. The results were/are higher costs and, in some cases, better treatment — but not necessarily.

"There is nothing inherent in the Ph.D., M.D., or M.S.W. that qualifies the individual as a good therapist nor is effective counseling limited to the practice of professionals . . ." *Journal of Professional Psychology,* 1978.

"There is more than ample evidence that persons from a broad range of backgrounds can supply effective counseling skills and apply them to the benefit of others." *Psychological Bulletin,* 1979.

Christian ministers over the years have provided most of the help for those who hurt . . . for good reason: 1) people know and trust their minister, 2) the counseling will not be counter to their value system, and 3) they can afford it because they will not be charged.

For decades research has indicated that the first counselor people are most likely to go to is their minister. The church has always been the most likely place to find compassion, care, and love. The church is available. The church has the facilities and the responsibility.

Interestingly, research shows that mental health groups are not always the most help to the sufferer.

Dr. Mansell Pattison found five kinds of psycho-health groups. Of these five, guess which provided the best therapy?

1. Self-Help Groups (like Alcoholics Anonymous)
2. Personal Interest Groups (like Parents Without Partners)
3. Social Interest Groups (barber shop quartets and church groups were put in the same classification)
4. Civic Groups (such as Rotary and Kiwanis)
5. Mental Health Groups

Dr. Pattison's research concluded that self-help groups like AA did the best work (85 percent therapeutically effective). The second most effective were the civic groups. Mental health groups were last.

The church can and does provide effective, successful therapy. The spiritual dimension provides the advantage. How? By providing the essential needs (spiritual and psychological) for maturity.

If a person has no sleep for a long period of time, he will hallucinate (see and/or hear things that are not really there). What needs treatment is not the symptom (hallucination) but the essential need (sleep). When adequate sleep is acquired, the hallucination disappears.

For years now, Dr. William Glasser has suggested that psychotherapists give too much attention to symptoms and not enough to the basic need underlying the symptom.

> Do these widely different behaviors indicate different
> psychiatric problems requiring a variety of explanations,
> or are they manifestations of one underlying difficulty?
> We believe that, regardless of how he expresses his

problem, everyone who needs psychiatric treatment suffers from one basic inadequacy: he is unable to fulfill his essential needs. The severity of the symptom reflects the degree to which the individual is unable to fulfill his needs. No one can explain exactly why one person expresses his problem with a stomach ulcer while another fears to enter an elevator; but whatever the symptom, it disappears when the person's needs are successfully fulfilled.

As a pecan tree without zinc produces weird pecans, so a child who grows up without certain psychological needs (love, for example) produces weird symptoms (such as withdrawal). The symptom, however, is not what needs the treatment but the missing essential need (love). When adequate love is supplied the withdrawal symptom disappears.

Following this reasoning I propose a thesis: that when the minister, through the word of God, supplies these basic essentials, people will need less counseling because they will have been fed a complete diet. Fewer serious abnormalities will appear. When they do, they will be easier to cure.

This approach is a preventative approach. Like dentistry or medicine, 80 percent of staying well is the practice of good health habits. It is easier to prevent lung cancer than to cure it after the diagnosis.

The Eight Essential Needs (Psychological/Spiritual) of Man

1. Identity

Eric Fromm, a noted psychologist, said: "Identity is so vital and imperative that man could not remain sane if he did not find some way of satisfying it." A decade ago there was an identity crisis among young university students — they were asking themselves questions like: "Who am I?" The counseling minister, through the Word, knows who a man is — even if the man doesn't know.

We are children of God made in His image (Genesis 1:26). We are here to glorify God by serving others (Galatians 5:13). We are going to a promised land far superior to this one (I Peter 1:1-5). The Christian receives his identity (as a child of God) and begins his inheritance (heaven) upon his conversion. When a person fully understands his potential as a child of God, nothing on earth will bind him anymore — he is a free man.

2. Faith

It is the nature of man to worship. If he doesn't find the true God he will worship false gods, the sun, or even things he makes with his own hands. It is man's nature to worship. He knows that something is not right without faith . . . Christianity supplies this essential need in its highest sense.

And moreover, faith guarantees power:

> Time would fail me to tell of Gideon, Barack, Samson, and Jephthah, of David and Samuel and the prophets — who through faith conquered kingdoms . . . received promises, stopped the mouths of lions, quenched raging fire, escaped the edge of the sword, won strength out of weakness, became mighty in word, put foreign armies to flight (Hebrews 11:31ff).

3. Hope

The basis for most depressions and suicides is despair and hopelessness . . . people have given up. Hope involves more than desire. Hope is desire plus expectation. Christ's blood supplies the reason for the expectation. His cross plus the Spirit's promise plus our faith kills despair and guarantees the joy of hope eternally.

4. Love

Love — the greatest healing agent in the world, is something that professional counselors cannot create nor release. Psychotherapy knows the healing power of love but finds itself unable to do much about it.

By contrast, Christianity extends a rule of life based wholly on love. "Beloved, let us love one another: for love is of God; and everyone that loveth is born of God, and knoweth God. He that loveth not knoweth not God: for God is love" (I John 4:7, 8).

One famous Harvard psychologist pointed out the sharp contrast between religion and psychology on this very issue:

> Perhaps the very insistence of religion in this matter is in part responsible for the "tenderness tabu" that has descended upon psychology. Having rejected the religious approach to the cure of souls, science regards it as more realistic to center attention upon . . . hate, aggression, compulsive sexuality . . . even if these are merely pathological conditions due to deprivation of love.

5. Community — Relationships — People

There are no happy hermits. People need people to make it. A study in Alameda, California, of 7,000 adults found that "friends can be good medicine." Its most dramatic finding was:

> Those people who had few social ties to others had a
> death rate two to five times higher than those who had
> strong social ties. Independent of whether they were
> smokers, drinkers, exercised, or overweight, this held
> for both sexes, all ethnic groups, rich and poor alike.

Where better to find true friends than in church, where the model of goodness died in service to others. Whose motto of social relations seems to be "serve one another in love" (Galatians 5:13). Ari Kieve, the psychiatrist, said: "There is a direct link between service to others and rewards in life."

6. Goals — Purpose — Meaning

Counselors have known for decades that when people have no direction in life it usually stems from no goals or no pursued goals.

"In my practice as a psychiatrist," says Ari Kieve, "I have found that helping people to develop personal goals has proved to the most effective way to help them cope with problems."

Purpose and goals give meaning to life. Jesus had one goal: to glorify the Father. As a little child, Jesus felt the need to be "about his Father's business." Twenty-one years later, His appointed task was complete when He uttered, "It is finished." He had lived His life for one worthy purpose. We would prosper if we would do the same thing.

7. Stable Values

The people of the United States have about twice the number of divorces as the next highest nation (Russia). We also have one of the highest rates of mental illness. This might relate to the fact that mankind operates from a value system. In the United States our values, for the most part, seem vague and shifting. When this is the case, direction in life tends to be the same.

To be mature, one must have a stable set of values. A person needs a value system that will stand the test of time, different cultures, and extreme circumstances. The Bible contains the only value system that measures up to these standards.

8. Forgiveness

Most important of all, mankind needs forgiveness. Guilt is a psychological fact. Counselors spend the majority of their time helping people overcome their guilt (real or imagined).

To deny the existence of guilt (and many counselors do) is to regulate man to the state of an animal. Christians believe that sin can be overcome only by God. God is anxious to forgive sins. Through Christ, He has promised absolute and eternal forgiveness to those who have sinned — no matter the degree.

To summarize, ministers have a lot going for them in the field of counseling.

1. Ministers are known and trusted by most everyone.

2. People know a minister will not devaluate Christian values.

3. People know that Christian counseling is affordable.

4. Ministers have answers to the essential needs of mankind.

5. The minister has (or should have) God's guidance and wisdom in prayer and in the Word.

21

Passages — A Way of Learning About God

KEN DYE

". . . but we have one who has been tempted in every way . . ."
(Hebrews 4:15)

It was in the latter stages of my undergraduate work at Abilene Christian College that a rather unusual event occurred which still brings a smile to my lips and an understanding to my heart. For several semesters I had taken courses from Dr. Frank Pack and, as a result of these years spent sitting at his feet, had learned much about this great man. As an undergraduate with a somewhat mediocre academic record, I was surprised to find that this distinguished Phi Beta Kappa always had time for me. Even though my questions were rather elemental and sometimes mundane, he would use each inquiry as an occasion to treat me with an elegance which I soon recognized to be a part of his everyday demeanor.

The event which stands out foremost in my mind took place during finals. For me, the two o'clock afternoon exam time for this last class with Dr. Pack was to be traumatic. There was so much to learn! I seemed to be so inadequate; and, in addition to this, the class was one which could also be taken for graduate credit, and those working toward their master's degrees seemed to be so capable. I knew that my exam would be read along with theirs, and I continued to grow more and more apprehensive.

Long before two o'clock arrived, I, along with the other students, was sitting in my seat with sweaty palms, a queasy stomach, and all the other symptoms characterizing pre-exam jitters, awaiting Dr. Pack's arrival. To my knowledge, he had never been late before; so he would walk in any second now, and then judgment. Two o'clock arrived and no Dr. Pack. 2:05, 2:10, 2:20, and still we continued to wait. Somewhere in the faint reaches of my memory, I recalled the regulations for awaiting the arrival of a Ph.D. I seemed to remember that after twenty minutes, walking out was permitted; but still I continued to sit. He had always seemed fair with me; and the only fair thing for me to do would be to remain. Perhaps something had happened?

Finally one of us went to call his home and, in a few minutes, the student returned saying that Dr. Pack would arrive momentarily. Minutes later, in walked Dr. Pack with no tie or coat (an indication of the rushed nature of his trip) while the class sat expectantly, wondering what had happened.

His response to this crisis is one which I have never forgotten. He made no excuses but simply said, "I was at home reading research papers, and I forgot the exam." He faced up to the situation and then went on to say, "You could have exercised your right to walk out, and there would have been no recourse; but because you were patient enough to wait, I will show my appreciation by giving you only half the exam."

I was ecstatic! The measure of mercy meted out by my teacher was probably the only thing that saved me in the class. I can't recall any of the questions and, now, some twenty-five years later, little of the class; but I do recall how a great man reacted to a fairly significant crisis, and that has lived on in my memory for these many years.

I have reflected often on the dynamics of this little episode and have come to see it as a reflection in miniature of just how God chooses to expose men and women to the realities of life. He permits each of us to function in time and space through the practical experiences which come into our everyday lives and then lets these teach lessons which we might not otherwise learn.

From Dr. Pack I learned much. At his discretion, inordinate power could have been wielded with no recriminations. However, he chose to deal gently; and then, when understanding was called for, gentleness was once again engaged. The lessons learned would be relived countless times, enabling me to comprehend more fully how God continues to deal with me.

Passages — God in History

Two thousand years ago, when God entered history in the person of His Son, Jesus Christ, He chose to face the experiences of life and to learn from them in the mode of a man. "For we do not have a high priest who is unable to sympathize with our weaknesses, but we have one who has been tempted in every way, just as we are — yet without sin. Let us then approach the throne of grace with confidence, so that we may receive mercy and find grace to help us in our time of need" (Hebrews 4:15-16).

Coming out of this divine decision are two realities — God's concern and God's understanding, and what a difference their appropriation can make in the struggles of human life. He became just as we are by nature so that we could believe with all our hearts that He knows from firsthand experience what our lives are like. We somehow feel closer to those who have walked where we are walking. We seem to trust most completely those who have experienced what we are experiencing.

Jesus was willing to accept the limitations which come with being human and to make the same walk that we are now walking. Therefore, He knows what it's like to be a child, an adolescent, and a man. In moving through these passages, He endured all the feelings which come from life, development, crises and then, death. God's choosing to teach men and women lessons from direct contact with each other while moving them through stages of life was also experienced by Jesus.

Just as it was important to God that in Jesus He would assimilate all the challenges of life, so it was important to God that we learn about Him through the practical experiences of life. Therefore, marriage, family life, and various other relational experiences are designed to teach us about God, and Him about us.

Passages — Marriage

In attempting to increase our understanding regarding submission to Christ, Paul in Ephesians, chapter 5, provides the analogy of marriage. The idea of wives submitting to husbands and husbands loving wives forces us to look to the practical for an insight into the spiritual. But Paul chooses to carry the analogy even further into a description of the church so that as the Scripture is ended, one is not easily able to discern at which point the discussion of marriage ends and the discussion of the church begins. The comparison seems to be so similar that they simply flow together and lose their individual identity.

"Wives, submit to your husbands as to the Lord. For the husband is the head of the wife as Christ is the head of the church . . ." (Ephesians 5:22).

"Husbands, love your wives, just as Christ loved the church and gave himself up for her" (Ephesians 5:25).

From the realities of marriage sometimes come lessons of mercy. It was Hosea who chose to marry one with a questionable reputation and then, after several children, watch as she turned from him to other lovers and finally, to open prostitution. Hosea reacted by proceeding to buy her back.

This love story is analogous to a deeper story — the saga of the living God and His relationship to the creation He has made. Hosea suggests that the way true lovers are with respect to the object of their affections is the way God is with us. Gomer had done it to Hosea; we have done it to God. Yet Hosea reached out to the non-repentant Gomer just as God continues to reach out to us. Our sins are never heinous enough to drive him away.

> How can I give you up, Ephraim?
> How can I hand you over, Israel?
> How can I treat you like Admah?
> How can I make you like Zeboiim?
> My heart is changed within me;
> All my compassion is aroused.
> I will not carry about my fierce anger,
> Nor devastate Ephraim again.
> For I am God and not man —
> The Holy One among you.
> I will not come in wrath (Hosea 11:8-9).

God chooses to move us through the journey of hard knocks; and with this journey, we learn firsthand about life. At each juncture, we are reminded that He too has walked this road. His method of teaching is through freedom of choice, but the road is one which has been carefully prepared from birth to death with each year numbered and no detours allowed.

Passages — Children

The journey begins with our being children, and it is then that authority is learned, along with many other lessons inherent in being under the directives of others. Attachment and disattachment are experienced; and without these, adulthood would be more difficult. Periodically, Jesus walks into view saying, "I know, I know."

"Remember when I was only 12 and my mother found me in the temple? She was wanting to protect me and hold me back, and I knew that I must break away. She knew of the dangers — I only knew of the mission" (Luke 2:41-52).

Passages — Adolescence

Because Jesus also walked through the teen years, He knows the feelings of being alone in a world full of changes. He, too, because of His manhood, had to face the challenges of choice. Do I preach? Should I remain a carpenter? Finally, the wilderness experience forced Him to decide between material privileges, fame, and glory, or power and domination (Matthew 4:1-11).

Passages — Adults

Jesus knows well our pressure as adults. He was literally overwhelmed on occasion when, in every direction He looked, there were those wanting a part of Him. Today the tugs from job, children, mate, social commitments, etc., are often unbearable; but He, too, felt those burdens. Often He would find it necessary to rid Himself of people for those precious moments of being alone with His father. He knows and He is sympathetic (John 14:13-14).

Passages — Death

With Jesus' dying at only 33 years of age, the most natural question to be asked is how can He be sympathetic to my growing old? In His prime He was taken away, so how can He be aware of what it is like for me at this point in my life?

In aging, one begins to know what it is like to be deserted and left alone, together with the problem of the lessening of physical strength.

Following the kiss in the garden, Jesus found that He had no one. He was forsaken and alone (Matthew 25:26). Upon the cross, His strength began to fade; and, in great despair, He cried out, "I thirst" (John 19:28).

Passages — The Here and Now

As the undulating brook, rippling and winding its way down the mountainside until it reaches the far expanse of the ocean, so my life continues to flow toward its end. Some twenty-five years ago, my mentor and friend touched my life, and I his. Time soon separated us, and we flowed in different directions; but because of our togetherness, we have learned about God from one another.

The brook continues to flow, but now my life touches others as Dr. Pack's touched mine. Those whom I meet respond in their various ways; but my prayer is that, in me, they might see God and that through these travels together, we might all learn a bit more.

Across the expanse of the universe come the resounding words, even more encouraging for now we know, "We do not have a high priest who is unable to sympathize with our weaknesses, but we have one who has been tempted in every way, just as we are — yet without sin." Let us then approach the throne of grace with CONFIDENCE.

22

The Power of Holding On to the Unseen

STEVEN LEMLEY

One of the most abstract renderings of the King James Bible is the great faith statement in Hebrews 11:1, "Now faith is the substance of things hoped for, the evidence of things not seen." Given the importance of the 11th chapter in preaching, it is helpful to hear the New International Version's substitution of "sure" and "certain" for "substance" and "evidence" in, "Now faith is being sure of what we hope for and certain of what we do not see."

Hebrews 11 is keyed off of 10:39, a great expression of confidence, "Now we are not of those who shrink back and are destroyed, but of those who believe and are saved." Faith is "what the ancients were commended for" (11:2), and the chapter makes clear the need to identify with them.

Many great Old Testament figures are mentioned but we will consider only four whose examples point out different qualities of faith, inspiring the same qualities in us. In order of appearance they are: Enoch (vv. 3-6), Noah (v. 7), Abraham (vv. 8-12, 17-19), and Moses (vv. 23-29). Then there is a larger group whose faith led to diverse outcomes (vv. 32-38). Focusing on these, we will know better what Alexander MacLaren called, "The Power of Holding On to the Unseen." God's power operates out of the realm of the unseen but becomes visible in His people, like the universe which was "formed at God's command, so that what is seen was not made out of what was visible" (v. 3).

Something from nothing, life from death, visible from invisible, power from weakness—this is the paradoxical way in which God has always acted, and still does, in His people.

Enoch's Faith

First, consider the glorious outcome of Enoch's quiet and impractical life. Enoch "could not be found, because God had taken him away" (v. 5). His was the faith of fellowship, constant devotion, resulting in uninterrupted life. By faith, he found God to be real and available to those who persistently seek Him. "Blessed are the pure in heart," Jesus said, "for they shall see God." This is the blessing of the single eye, the eye whose desire is intense and pointed and wants the experience of God Himself.

In Enoch's case, this blessing was continuing and final. His quest for fellowship pleased God so that Enoch did not face the death which all mortals anticipate.

We all need to have the quality of Enoch's faith in our hypertensive world. Jesus said to Martha, and to us, "You are anxious for many things but one thing is really important" (Luke 10:41,42), and that one thing, fellowship with God, is the point around which our lives should be organized. One said, "I'm too busy not to pray" but too many of us exist only according to a principle of life which crowds out prayer. If we ask, then we may fail to go on to thanking, interceding, and praising where Enoch and many like-minded people have found God.

Like Enoch, by faith, we seek to live in fellowship with God so that we will ultimately find Him. Hold on to the unseen—there is the power!

Noah's Faith

Out of faith and fear, Noah followed God's instructions to "build an ark to save his family." It must have come as a disappointment to Noah to know his life's work was to do something for which there was no precedent and no apparent need. He looked ridiculous and he was ridiculed. But how could his neighbors help it? They were hardened to God. If God had spoken to them, they could not have heard, indeed, they did not hear Him speak through Noah; the world around did not respond to his preaching, his faith, or his obedience to God. They found only condemnation.

There is always something in faith which appears ridiculous to a faithless world. In our time, one need only look to print and broadcast media where Christian morality is depicted as unrealistic or oppressive and where the obedient life is seen as wasted. This is emotional persecution of the kind Noah experienced.

By faith, with Noah, we hold on to the unseen in the face of ridicule or being ignored. We find the power to build faith in our families, churches, and communities while we wait for God to work out the world's destiny.

Abraham's Faith

The theme of faith is found in Abraham as he followed God to adventure into the unknown, saw the beginning of God's promise to mankind played out in the birth of a son of promise to parents who were old, then obeyed God to sacrifice that son — all by faith.

With all his humanity, we stand in reverence before the faith of this one who left a greater center of civilization for the life of a bedouin. As this man of wealth and influence left his city, someone might have asked, "Why? Why leave this place of safety and comfort, beauty and culture, education and growth for something unknown, unseen, and likely difficulty?" Abraham might have answered, "This place with its great walls and mighty buildings will one day vanish under tons of earth. Scholars will debate is existence. Archaeologists will finally dig to prove that this city ever existed. I'm looking for something with greater permanence, created and sustained by God." And so Abraham went out, finding permanence in a nomadic life of faith.

He experienced wonderful things, God's promise fulfilled, the growth of his faith to believe that God could raise the dead which motivated his obedience in his beginning to sacrifice Isaac.

The power and permanence in Abraham's life came from holding on to the unseen as he waited for God to fulfill a great promise in founding a people for His purpose. Whatever the world holds out as permanent disappears quickly but "Jesus Christ is the same yesterday and today and forever" (Hebrews 13:8).

The Faith of Moses

The story of Moses begins with the faith of parents who saw something wonderful in him and preserved him from the wrath of the king. The faith of Moses' parents preserved him, and we should be thankful when parents bring their children to faith. We sometimes discount the child who is baptized into Christ in our church growth statistics: "Forty people were baptized in this church last year, but half of them were the children of members." Actually, we should praise God that Christian homes are bringing along young Christians and starting them on the path to spiritual maturity. When a child comes to Christ, we see the potential in his life and believe in the unseen hand of God to bring out all that the child can be.

Then, we see that Moses gave up wealth, power, and pleasure in exchange for mistreatment among his true heritage—the people of God. He left Egypt, kept the Passover, led the people safely through the sea, all because "he saw Him who is invisible" (v. 27).

Moses' faith is the faith of one who used his position, gifts, influence in God's service—he was not too proud to use his great resources in obedient service to God.

Faith in Faith vs. Faith in God

We live by faith at many levels. Just getting through a day requires every person's putting some confidence in things unseen. Even walking is a process which can only be done when we keep slightly off-balance, leaning into the unknown.

Faith is a popular subject nowadays. Popular faith is not, however, the kind of faith we find in Hebrews 11. Today's brand of faith is instrumental: believe in God, believe in yourself. Believe in your cause and you'll get what you want.

But what about the believers in Hebrews 11? Did they get what they wanted? The answer is surprising and disappointing to one who wants faith to always lead to success and personal fulfillment. "All these people were still living by faith when they died. They did not receive the things promised: they only saw them and welcomed them from a distance. And they admitted that they were aliens and strangers on earth" (v. 13). Again, "These were all commended for their faith, yet none of them received what had been promised" (v. 29). Of course, they were looking forward to the promised Messiah—a deliverer for the nation, a redeemer. But He did not come in their lifetimes—they died in faith that He would come. And yet, they kept on believing!

Many are interested in what faith can do right now. If I visualize, imagine, believe strongly enough, I can get what I want. But when faith is reduced to that, it is faith in faith, not faith in God. Faith in faith can lead to loss of faith in God altogether.

The Outcome of Faith in God

By contrast, "Whoever watches the wind will not plant; whoever looks at the clouds will not reap. As you do not know the path of the wind, or how the body is formed in a mother's womb, so you cannot understand the work of God, the Maker of all things."

"Sow your seed in the morning, and at evening let not your hands be idle, for you do not know which will succeed, whether this or that, or whether both will do equally well" (Ecclesiastes 11:5, 6).

Believe in God to bring about His purposes for you. There is great adventure, sometimes joy and sometimes sorrow, in the real life of faith.

In this life, the result of faith in God may be apparent success or apparent failure. Success and failure are not the issue — holding on to the unseen is the point. Look at Gideon, Barak, Samson, Jephtah, David, Samuel, the prophets (vv. 32-38). Some seemed to succeed, some seemed to fail, most had a dramatic mixture of success and failure. Some conquered kingdoms, did acts of righteousness, obtained promises, defeated wild animals, overcame fire and sword, drew strength out of weakness, put armies to flight, saw life given back to the dead. *But others who also believed* were tortured, mocked, scourged, imprisoned, stoned, sawed in two, tempted, killed, poor, abused, and homeless. Same faith, everybody believing, but a wide spectrum of results is here.

Someone said, "There are two tragedies in life. One is to fail to get what you want. The other is to get it." The life of faith puts its focus on God, not on fears or things desired, and so is a victorious life in celebration and in sorrow.

Our Faith

God wants people who believe in Him, who think He is there, and who want Him in control. With that faith, what a difference can come into a life, what power will be in the church!

With that kind of faith, we can all take our places among the faithful in Hebrews 11. By faith we will stay married and keep our families together, take a job for greater service, leave a temptation behind, keep loving and praying for a wayward child, build up the church instead of criticize, serve the spirit of God instead of the senses, remain undisturbed by the unbelief or mockery of unbelievers. And by faith, the church will look not only to its rising statistics or diminishing membership, not only to its organization or lack of it, but will place its hope in God alone. We will live contrary to this age of sight and know the power of holding on to the unseen.

This is no time to grow weak or lose hope. This is the time to look to the unseen for power, "since we are surrounded by such a great cloud of witnesses, let us throw off everything that hinders and the sin that so easily entangles, and let us run with perseverance the race marked out for us. Let us fix our eyes on Jesus, the author and perfecter of our faith, who for the joy set before Him endured the cross, scorning its shame, and sat down at the right hand of the throne of God. Consider Him who endured such opposition from sinful men, so that you will not grow weary and lose heart.'

There is power in holding on to the unseen.

23

First-Century Evangelism Today

SILAS SHOTWELL

The church has lost the secret of first-century evangelism. This is evidenced by the lack of New Testament growth. We do not think in terms of "multitudes" being converted. At best we have "additions" but never "multiplications." Our minds cannot conceive a present-day Pentecost where three thousand would be baptized at one time.

Excuses for our present impotence are legion. Times have changed, denominationalism has counterfeited true Christianity, people are too prosperous, Christians are not as committed, etc. But somehow, excuses do not suffice. There must have been problems in the first century too. The world was still the world, Christians were Christians, the gospel was the gospel. Why the change? What would first-century Christians do if given our time and place? Could they still reach multitudes? Could they do an even better job with the added help of printing presses, radio, television, telephones, and rapid means of travel?

What would have happened in the first century if they had relied on pulpit sermons on evangelism, personal work training classes, charts and filmstrips, door-to-door campaigns, and committees? In Acts 8:4 "they that were scattered abroad went everywhere preaching the word." In verse one we are told that this scattering did not include the apostles.

In other words, the "professionals" stayed home, and the "members" preached wherever they went. That is not the way things are done today. The failure to somehow motivate and train members has resulted in the lack of growth in the church.

"Personal work" has become a work for professionals. It has its own language with terms like "cottage meetings," "prospects," "closing the sale." The stereotyped personal worker must be a student of human nature as well as the word. He must know the enemy and therefore have a thorough knowledge of denominations, cults, and virtually every "ism." He must be skilled in argument so as to stay on the offensive and adequately stand up for the truth. He must also be a first-rate salesman. His persuasive ability must be surpassed only by his unending reserve of memorized proof texts.

It is no wonder that so few people in the church talk to others about the gospel. "I am not a salesman." "I am not a theologian." "I don't know enough." These statements may be honest reactions to an overemphasis on professionalism. Those New Testament Christians who went "everywhere preaching the word" were not professionals. But they went. They taught. And they helped to spread the borders of the kingdom. In order to restore New Testament growth, we must begin a fearless reexamination of New Testament principles of growth. We must be willing to change our approach.

Three pertinent questions need to be asked in New Testament evangelism:

1. What kind of MEN were they?
2. What was their MESSAGE?
3. What were their METHODS?

What Kind of Men Were They?

Jesus began the expansion of His ministry by calling four fishermen. He said to them, "Follow me, and I will make you fishers of men" (Matthew 4:19). It is significant that when Jesus called men who were later to be apostles He did not select them from the priests, the Levites, or the Sanhedrin. He chose common men rather than professionals. He chose ignorant men rather than scholars. He chose them, not for what they were, but for what He could make them.

Throughout Jesus' ministry He worked with the common. He used children to teach disciples, a Samaritan woman to teach her friends, and a cured demoniac to teach a city. Even when a scholar like Paul entered God's ministry, he spoke not "with excellency of speech or of wisdom" but he came in "weakness, and in fear, and in much trembling" (I Corinthians 2:1, 3).

Those who went "everywhere preaching the word" were also common people. It was not their own strength, but God's, that enabled them to turn the world upside down.

Preachers and personal work directors alone will never win the world to Christ. They have a unique, equipping ministry, but it is the average Christian who has the best opportunity to teach the lost. The church is most thoroughly the church when it touches the world. The gospel must be taught across backyard fences, in factories, in classrooms, and in garden clubs.

Members of the church are strategically located. Their daily example and words appropriately spoken when God opens a door of opportunity will reach more of the lost than will be reached from pulpits. If the world is to be shaken with the gospel, it will be when people from all walks of life do what they can where they are.

Put yourself in the place of the lost person. To whom would you listen? Would it be to the glib clergy-scholar-salesman who answers your questions before you even ask them and knows your needs better than you know them? Or would it be to the unpretentious friend who has gained your trust through his own example and simply shares with you what faith in God means to him?

God wants men today who are more aware of their own weaknesses than their strengths. He wants men who know that "of their own selves they can do nothing" (John 5:30) but who also know they can "do all things through Christ which strengthens" (Philippians 4:13). When people put themselves in God's hands He will use them.

First-century evangelists were common people who put their trust in God. The same kind of people are needed today.

What Was Their Message?

When Paul went to Corinth he determined to know nothing but "Jesus Christ, and Him crucified" (I Corinthians 2:2). He did not want the Corinthian's faith to "stand in the wisdom of men, but in the power of God" (I Corinthians 2:5). To the Romans he said that the gospel of Christ was "the power of God unto salvation, to everyone that believeth; to the Jew first, and also to the Greek" (Romans 1:16).

What is contained in that gospel? First-century growth cannot be hoped for without a first-century message.

The word "gospel" means "good news." Good news is easy to tell. Everyone likes to tell about a new grandchild, a raise in pay, a clean bill of health from a medical checkup. The good news of the gospel is far greater than these things. It tells what God has done for man through Christ.

Paul's definition of the gospel is in I Corinthians 15:1-11. The essence of it is that "Christ died for our sins, according to the Scriptures; and that He was buried, and that He rose again the third day, according to the Scriptures (I Corinthians 15:3, 4).

The simple message of God's grace led thousands on Pentecost to say "what shall we do?" Response to this good news enabled the Ethiopian eunuch to go on his way rejoicing. It caused the course of Paul's life to be completely changed.

The very nature of the good news perhaps motivated multitudes of first-century Christians to go "everywhere preaching the word." Perhaps the lack of such a message today is one of the primary reasons why more people are not evangelists.

Many of us have replaced the "good news" with "bad news." Instead of joyfully announcing to the world what God has done through Christ, we have scolded the world for its weakness and sin without ever offering a solution. Rather than lighting a candle, we have cursed the darkness. Still others of us have replaced the "good news" with "good views." We have relied on logic and philosophy instead of the simple power of God's saving gospel. We have tried to reason people into the kingdom of God. We have implied that becoming a Christian is accepting a list of doctrines rather than responding to God's love.

The first-century message was a message of good news. The same kind of message is needed today.

What Were Their Methods?

Today we are often method-oriented. "How to" books are usually best-sellers. When someone else is successful we want to know their techniques.

One of the reasons our evangelism has been inadequate is because we have been too concerned with methods and not as interested in men or message. Our personal work training classes have stressed mechanics. We have outfitted evangelists with paraphernalia and outlines . . . and failed. There are people who have a roomful of projectors, charts, and diagrams, but have never led one person to Christ.

On the other hand, picture the average new convert. He is happy, excited, running over. In his feeble and untrained way he tells people about his new discovery. Without training, without a method, he does what we are unable to force people to do. His is a sharing process rather than one of selling or debating. When one has something to share he will share it. If he does not, all the training in the world will not help.

The truth needs to be proclaimed more than it needs to be defended. It can defend itself. The message will provide methods. When one is filled with the good news of the gospel he will overflow.

Sharing the gospel is not like selling insurance. It is not like defending the Democratic platform over the Republican. It is not like contrasting Adventism and Mormonism.

When Jesus came, "the Word became flesh and dwelt among us, full of grace and truth" (John 1:14). In a sense this is what must happen with us. We are touched with the gospel message. We respond. We are transformed. We proclaim. We do not boast of ourselves, but of the word and of its power.

The non-formal, non-argumentive, personal profession of faith is the most powerful proclamation of the Word. Our own attitudes and lives underline the truth of what we say.

It is premature to emphasize methods without first emphasizing the message and the messenger. We will not create evangelists with methods. When a person does not share Christ, he needs more than a method. When a congregation is not evangelizing it needs more than a program.

The first-century method was sharing. The same method is needed today. The challenge for today's church is to put our trust in the simplicity and power of the first-century gospel. With the conviction that it is still "the power of God unto salvation," we will share it with fantastic results.

24

The Perpetual Restoration

JIMMY JIVIDEN

The 19th century Restoration Movement on the American frontier has a close relationship to those who are members of the church of Christ today. But the Restoration Movement is not the church of Christ. The Restoration Movement is a time-bound, culturally oriented, and man-led historical phenomenon through which the church of Christ in the United States came into being. It is not to be identified with Jesus' church which is an eternal kingdom, a people above cultural and ethnic division and led by Jesus Christ Himself.

The 19th and 20th century Restoration Movement identified with the church of Christ in the United States is one of many restoration movements in history. It is one of many such movements which have spontaneously arisen in different nations of the world. It is one of many contemporary movements which in one way or another gives allegiance to the Restoration Principle. The church of Christ is not unique in claiming roots in a restoration movement.

What then is the relationship of the 19th century Restoration Movement to the identity and existence of the church of Christ today?

There is a historical relationship. The 19th century movement provides roots into the past and connects to men who were striving to restore the New Testament church. The battles they fought, the victories they won, and the defeats they suffered enable us to see more clearly the task of restoring New Testament Christianity.

There is a philosophical relationship. A Restoration Principle connects the 19th century Restoration Movement with contemporary churches of Christ. This Restoration Principle can perhaps best be stated in this way:

> . . . striving to be and become the ideal church as
> reflected in the New Testament.

This statement has no subject and hence is not identified with a limited historical movement.

This statement shows that reality always falls behind the ideal. Even the New Testament churches like Jerusalem, Ephesus, and Corinth were not perfect. They were not the ideal but reflected the ideal to the degree that they followed the teaching of Jesus Christ.

This statement shows the task of restoration is never complete. People seeking to please Christ will always be "striving to be and become." They never come to a point in life that they know all truth, practice perfect moral conduct, or attain absolute spiritual worship. To be and become the church of Christ in the 20th century there must be a Perpetual Restoration.

The Restoration Principle was the means by which the Restoration Movement came into being. By this movement the New Testament church of Christ has been able to exist after the New Testament pattern. The church of Christ will continue to exist only if there is a Perpetual Restoration. The accumulated traditions of men must continue to be recognized and removed. The approved New Testament practices which have been neglected because of the frailty of man must be accepted and practiced in the life of the church if the church of Christ is to exist in our time and in this place.

There are two dangers to be avoided in considering the Restoration Principle.

The first is to regard the restoration of New Testament Christianity as an impossible task in the 20th century and give up the quest. This has been done by the majority of professing Christians. They are satisfied with maintaining the status quo of their denominational creeds and human traditions.

The second danger is to regard the restoration of New Testament Christianity as a completed task. This has been done by those who hid their heads in the sand and childishly believe they have reached the impossible dream of restoring every jot and tittle of the New Testament church. This is willful ignorance and inexcusable pride.

The Jews Paul addressed in Romans 2:17-23 did not see the importance of Perpetual Restoration. They trusted in their historical roots going back to Abraham (Matthew 3:9). They trusted in those bits of Scriptures they carried in their phylacteries (Matthew 23:5). They desired a knowledge of the law by which they condemned others but refused to practice the law themselves.

> But if you bear the name "Jew," and rely upon the law, and boast in God, and know His will, and approve the things that are essential, being instructed out of the law, and are confident that you yourself are a guide to the blind, a light to those who are in darkness, a corrector of the foolish, a teacher of the immature, having in the law the embodiment of knowledge and of the truth; you therefore who teach another, do you not teach yourself? You who preach that one should not steal, do you steal? You who say that one should not commit adultery, do you commit adultery? You who abhor idols, do you rob temples? You who boast in the law, through your breaking the law, do you dishonor God?

The Jews Paul addressed had to learn that their salvation did not rest upon ethnic roots of the historical past or propositional truth found in some proof texts they carried on their arms or foreheads. Salvation could only come through grace by faith in Jesus Christ. They needed a personal confrontation to shatter their trust in self and restore the faith by which Abraham attained righteousness (Romans 4:1-3).

There is always a tension between the real and the ideal in the dynamics of restoring New Testament Christianity. The church is restored and at the same time is in the process of being restored. The existence of fornicators, parties, idol worshippers, and gross immaturity in the church at Corinth did not keep Paul from calling them the church of God. Neither does a few old soreheads, a couple of hypocrites, and a bunch of immature Christians keep the church of Christ in the 20th century from being God's people.

This tension between the real and the ideal is expressed by Paul in a personal way (Philippians 3:12):

"Not that I have already obtained it, or have already become perfect, but I press on . . ."

Paul said that he was not perfect.

Notice verse 15:

"Let us therefore, as many as are perfect, have this attitude . . ."

In verse 12 he said that he was not perfect. In verse 15 he suggests that he is perfect. What is the difference?

The word translated "perfect" means "mature," not sinless perfection. Paul had reached some of his goals. He had attained a certain stage of maturity. In this sense he could be considered perfect. Paul had not attained all of his ideals and was still pressing on toward the goal. He still had some maturing to do. He was still not perfect.

A 21-year-old man is mature, but he still has some growing to do to be mature. In the same way, the restoring of the church of Christ in the 20th century is a reality. But who will deny that there is still some restoring to do?

The church of Christ today must continue the Perpetual Restoration if it is to be identified with the ideal church as reflected in the New Testament. This can be done by following a basic methodology outlined in a popular restoration slogan of the past:

Speak where the Bible speaks and be silent where the Bible is silent.

There must be a return to the Scriptures. The word of God is the seed of the kingdom. It is the standard to follow in all things pertaining to the faith and practice by those who follow Christ. The Scriptures are the absolute "once-for-all" norm.

The word of God has always been at the very heart of people returning to God. The Old Testament prophets spoke the word of God to recall ancient Israel to God. It was the finding of the "book of the law" in the temple in the days of Josiah that began a restoration in his day (II Kings 22). It was the reading of the law of Ezra that began a restoration after the return from Babylon. Jesus constantly called men back to the Scriptures.

The first and most fundamental part of maintaining a Perpetual Restoration is to focus on the knowing, the understanding, the believing, and the obeying of the Scriptures.

There must be a cutting away of human traditions. Whatever is practiced in the name of Jesus Christ must have a "thus saith the Lord" for it. This is what is meant by the phrase "be silent where the Bible is silent." If the Scriptures are silent about a thing, then it must be cut off. It cannot be a part of the restored life and teachings of the church.

This includes creeds — both written and unwritten. This includes traditions and time-honored customs. It was such traditions that Jesus condemned in Matthew 15:6:

". . . you invalidated the word of God for the sake of your traditions."

Cutting off human traditions has always been a painful discipline in the Restoration Movement. Feelings are often hurt. churches are sometimes split. Souls are sometimes lost because of the inability to see the difference between the word of God and the traditions of men.

There must be a renewed practice of that which has been neglected. Whatever is taught in the Scriptures which has been neglected or rejected in the past must be affirmed and practiced in the Perpetual Restoration. This is what is meant by the phrase "speak where the Bible speaks." This was demonstrated in the restoration which occurred during the times of Josiah and Ezra. In both incidents the Passover had been neglected with the passing of time. In both incidents the Passover began to be practiced again after the word of God was read.

Restoration is positive as well as negative. It is building up as well as tearing down. It is not enough to be against the innovations of men. One must also be for all things which have been commanded of the Lord. Those involved in the Perpetual Restoration must not only be known for what they are against, but they must also affirm and practice the positive teachings of the Scriptures.

Only by a diligent involvement in the Perpetual Restoration will the 20th century church of Christ keep from evolving into a denomination of men. Every aspect of social conformity, every element of human pride, and every deception of false religion combine to pull men away from the restoration ideal. The church is always only one generation away from apostasy. All it would take for the church of Jesus Christ to become just another institution of men is for one generation to neglect the Restoration Principle.

There are tendencies from two directions to "denominationalize the church" in our time.

On one hand there are those who no longer recognize the divine nature of the church because they have rejected the Restoration Principle. They view the church of Christ as just another denomination among denominations. They ridicule the ideal that the church of the New Testament could be restored as a naive fantasy. They make puns of "church of Christism." Through this bold front of criticism, one can sometimes see the glimmer of hurt and pain that is felt by the critic. Often they are wallowing in the rubble of their own shattered faith. They feel despair because of the spiritual vacuum left from their lost ideals.

On the other hand there are those who are contributing to the denominationalizing of the church from the opposite extreme. They claim to accept the Restoration Principle. They are loyal in doctrine and practice to the established patterns of conduct in the brotherhood. Their view of the church is denominational. Often they are second- and third-generation Christians who have accepted without question that which has been handed down from their fathers. They are not concerned so much with "speaking where the Bible speaks" as they are with maintaining the status quo. They reject error because their fathers did, not because they have tested it by the Scriptures. They are loyal to the truth because "that is the way it has always been done." They sometimes even call themselves "church of Christers." God has no grandchildren. Every person comes to his own faith. Every person is responsible for his own practice.

These extremes feed on each other and find support from each other as they battle each other. Both are forces which will humanize the church of Christ.

I challenge you to keep on restoring the church of the New Testament. The Restoration Movement is still unfinished. It always will be until Jesus comes.

Members of the church of Christ must always be open to learn truth which they had not known before . . . if that truth is grounded in the Scriptures. Members of the church of Christ must always be willing to change . . . if that change is in the direction of the teachings of the Scriptures. By so doing, the church will remain free from the bondage of ecclesiastical domination. By so doing the church will not stagnate into a denomination of men. By so doing the church will be and become the church of Christ reflected in the New Testament.

A statement by Paul in Philippians 3:13-14 expresses the spirit of the Perpetual Restoration:

". . . Forgetting what lies behind and reaching forward to what lies ahead, I press on toward the goal . . ."

May such always be our prayer, our plan, and our practice.

25

This Will Be the End of Us!

BILL LOVE

He left his pocket-sized New Testament on a muddy battlefield in Vietnam. A scribbled inscription read: "Thelma, I want you to have my Bible. Maybe it'll remind you of me when you use it. I'm sure God will take care of you. He always takes care of His own children, even if it's His will that we die . . . See you at home, Larry."

What strange words! "God will take care of His children . . . even if it is His will that we die!" Was this meant to be consolation? Many would say, "What kind of God is this? Could He not prevent a young man's death and return him to his loved ones?"

For centuries Christians have confessed faith in this God. Have we been fools? We need answers to this question, for ourselves and our children. Few of us will ever know the life and death battlefield situation. We are "up against it" in other ways. Someone we counted on let us down. Financial calculations proved wrong and we face bankruptcy. Unresolved marital conflict may end in divorce. A few cells in the body ran amuck, terminal cancer. In larger scope, our whole civilization lives under a mushroom-shaped cloud. As one man who rode the rails during our Great Depression observed, "There are lots of things that can put a man on the fritz!"

So quickly the earth may shift beneath our feet! Without notice we can find ourselves in the depths. When this happens we may want to say, "This will be the end of us! Where is God now?"

In times like these we could use a faith like Larry's. Where did he get the peace to write so calmly about death and God's love for His children? How could he spend his last hours concerned for Thelma? What accounts for his almost nonchalant confidence?

Without a doubt Larry found his hope in that New Testament. Perhaps he had read the words of another young man who died thinking of God and about others. To His followers Jesus said: ". . . some of you they will put to death . . . but not a hair of your head will perish" (Luke 21:16-18). There it is again, that paradoxical faith! What does he mean, ". . . they will put you to death . . . but not a hair of your head will perish"?

Jesus wanted His disciples braced for things to come. The twelve had no idea how tough life could get. Their candidate for Messiah would be brutally put down, and with Him their most cherished dreams. And it would not end there. For His sake they would be called on the carpet, grilled, even put to death. Jerusalem itself would fall. The city of God razed by the unbelieving Romans! Struggling for balance and meaning, they would often feel despair. "This will be the end of us! Where is God now?"

If Jesus knew all this beforehand, how could He expect His disciples to find peace? There must be a secret here, something He knew we have yet to learn.

Jesus Was A Realist About Life

He gave no easy answers, simple formulas, or catchy mottos for troubled times. Jesus was on His way to the cross. No "power of positive thinking" could prevent it. Events were set in motion. Neither heaven nor hell would avert the outcome. In exorcising demons, Jesus had announced the arrival of God's kingdom in power (Luke 11:20). He came to do battle with Satan. Now He was locked in mortal combat with the powers of darkness. Someone would get hurt before this was over.

The disciples also remained vulnerable. Jesus did not say, "Tell my story, if you get your approach and method right the world will love you." He knew better. Even less would Jesus teach a macho self-reliance: "When the going gets tough, the tough get going." Jesus knew when the going got tough enough, the tough would crater. Slogans and mottos fall short. When Christians die for their faith and Jerusalem falls to the pagans, no one wants to hear: "Not to worry. Time heals all wounds."

When the chips are down, what is more maddening than a cockeyed optimist? What sells automobiles and toothpaste falls somewhat short in a cancer hospital. Jesus knew the score. He did not mock their fears by games of make-believe.

Jesus told it like it would be. "Nation will rise against nation. . . there will be great earthquakes, and in various places famines and pestilences; and there will be terrors and great signs from heaven. But before all this they will lay their hands on you and persecute you, delivering you up to the synagogues and prisons, and you will be brought before kings and governors for my name's sake . . . You will be delivered up even by parents and brothers and kinsmen and friends, and some of you they will put to death; you will be hated by all for my name's sake."

God's "Nevertheless"

But that was not all, Jesus added, "But not a hair of your head will perish. By your endurance you will gain your lives." This reminds us of the psalms of lament where some poor, bedeviled soul cried out to God from the depths. Then, before the psalm was over, came those words of hope: "but God" or "nevertheless." Even from the pit the psalmist saw God's rescue. It was God's "nevertheless."

Jesus saw what lay ahead as hard, cold reality. But not final reality. While He never underrated Satan, Jesus always remembered His Father's power. If God wills, even death is not fatal.

The problem is that we tend to see life only in terms of our "three score and ten." Believing that all loose ends will be tied up before we die, we smile bravely and say, "all's well that ends well." Jesus worked with a much longer time frame. Our end is not God's deadline, our limits are not His boundaries.

God sometimes gives alarming comfort. Jesus said to persecuted Christians in Asia, "Be faithful unto (up until and including) death, and I will give you the crown of life." Every moment we live God preserves our lives. One day He will not. Nevertheless, life and death both remain within His power. "Whether we live or die we are the Lord's." Episodes from the gospels illustrate. While Jesus slept on a cushion, the boat tossing on the sea, His disciples grew frantic. "Don't you care if we perish?!" He calmed the sea, and then His disciples. The God of all Creation spoke and the sea hushed. Rescue was the divine plan for this moment.

On another occasion when they were all in the same boat, Jesus would not calm the sea. They bailed out on Him. He went down along with the ship, saying, "Father, into Thy hands I commit my spirit." That could mean resurrection from death or "This is the end of me!" Either way, He left it to His Father.

Sometimes God stills the storm. On other occasions He calms our hearts even in the raging tempest. But there remains a third possibility. The waves may overwhelm us, we may go down with the ship. Even then, God retains His sovereign control. He can bring us back to life from the depths. This third method is our least favorite. Ironically, here lies the ultimate security of our lives: God's "neverthless."

And Sure Enough

As Jesus said, things went from bad to worse. Luke says in the next chapter, ". . . and Satan entered the heart of Judas." Then Peter, oblivious to Jesus' briefing, took matters into his own hands. He tried to decapitate a servant of the high priest and was rebuked for his frantic heroics. Then Jesus said something to the arresting crowd that tells us this was more than a church fuss among first-century Jews. Something ominous was going on behind conflicting psychologies, class struggles, and theological differences. To His enemies Jesus said, "But this is your hour, and the power of darkness" (Luke 22:53).

We notice that Jesus consciously chose to enter this desperate battle between God and Satan. Do we also see why He did it? It was our battle, Jesus is there for us. An old spiritual asks, "Were you there when they crucified my Lord?" We were there. For us Jesus took on the dark forces of hell.

Obviously, Satan won. The crucifixion settled matters for everyone. The Roman soldiers finished another day's work. Jerusalem's religious leaders had defused a dangerous situation and preserved their control. And the disciples? "So much for Camelot! This will be the end of us! Where is God now?"

Nevertheless, what appeared to be the end was only a beginning. God raised Jesus from the depths. Two disciples on the Emmaeus road failed to recognize Jesus walking with them. "We thought," they said wistfully, "that He was the one . . ." The news was too good to be true! Still bleeding inside, the disciples were wary of resurrection rumors. But Jesus appeared, confirmed the rumors, and shared their tears of joy. Then, He sent them out to tell the story. (End of Luke's volume one.)

(Volume two continues.) The disciples' test was coming. Jesus said they would be His witnesses in Jerusalem, Judea, and to the uttermost parts of the earth. Peter could have objected. "Lord, do you think that is wise? Beginning right here in Jerusalem before the dust settles?" A fair question. How did the infant church survive in this city which crucified Jesus less than six weeks before?

Satan viciously attacked the believers both from without and within. Annas, Caiaphas, and their crowd were determined not to let this stubborn fanaticism get out of hand. Adjustments within the new fellowship were difficult and explosive. More than once the community could have come apart at the seams. God's church was born in dark days, times when disciples could have said, "This will be the end of us! Where is God now?"

Luke tells how they won. In obedience to Jesus, they waited and prayed. God triumphed in His Spirit: creating life, nurturing His people, controlling events. They continued in bold proclamation, prayer, fellowship, breaking bread together. God won! The fledgling community of believers enjoyed the victory.

Nothing could stop God's kingdom! What began in Bethlehem reached Rome itself! This gospel first proclaimed to Jews was preached among the Gentiles! God's mission of salvation apparently doomed on Golgotha forged ahead with a broken, remade Pharisee Christian named Paul.

But let us remember the dark days. We read Paul's words, "We know that in everything God works for good with those who love Him..." How easily this can mean that God protects us from all suffering here and now! If that is so, how could Jesus have died on the cross? Stephen dies at the hands of the most religious people in town, in a stone quarry. The sword of a petty king took the life of James. After writing his epistle of joy, Paul went under the executioner's axe. The here and now can be a bloody place to live. In total honesty Jesus tells it like it is. Then He adds God's "nevertheless."

This is Our Story

Bad things happen, not only to good people, but to God's people. Our lives are spent in search of security. We gauge the safety levels as we go by various instruments. Some of us trust our feelings. Others rely on their knowledge. Action is the answer for many. In the last analysis, none of these yardsticks is dependable. Our feelings may be wrong, Judas felt betrayed by God and that he had to betray Jesus. Our knowledge stands suspect, "we know in part." The Scribes and Pharisees knew perfectly well, by Moses' law, that Jesus was a blasphemer deserving death. Our action is often as misguided as Peter's swordwork in the garden. What a cruel surprise to discover that our instruments have been faulty, self-reliant security an illusion! Nothing we feel, know, or do can safeguard our existence. We must look elsewhere.

Elie Wiesel stood incredulous with hundreds of other Jews in a concentration camp. They watched as three innocent teenagers were hanged for a boyish prank. Someone said, "Where is God now?!" After a chilling silence another answered, "He is there on the gallows with them!" The confessor must have been living in the twenty-third psalm. "Yea, though I walk through the valley of the shadow of death I will fear no evil for thou are with me!" Notice the sure ground of confidence. The psalmist did not say, "I will fear no evil because I feel good about it, I know the purpose of it all, I will act the man!" He looked away from himself to Another present on the scene. "I will fear no evil for Thou art with me."

If a psalmist knew this God before Golgotha and the open tomb, how much more should we know His steadfast love in our lives today!

Larry knew Jesus. He knew His Lord went down to death, that God raised him up! Jesus' presence on that battlefield filled Larry's heart and enabled him to write, "He takes care of His children . . . even if it is His will that we die."

In 1960 I sat with other students in Dr. Frank Pack's study of Revelation. His great learning and insight inspired me. He made us want to study and learn. But he did more. He revealed Revelation to us, its central theme. Christians under persecution feared what the emperor Domitian might have up his sleeve. God gave John a vision. The curtain of heaven was drawn back. Seated there in Control Central of all creation is God Himself! Here is the final truth. Our lives are not determined in Jerusalem or Rome, in Washington or Moscow. We are not doomed by what was, is, or may be in the here and now.

Under fear of persecution Christians in Asia were ready to say, "This will be the end of us! Where is God now?" John answers, "No, this is *not* the end of you, it is your *beginning*! Observe the Lamb beside the throne. For you He was slain, for you He lives! Worthy is He to be praised forevermore. Do you see the One who rules, sitting upon the throne? He has never lost control. Not for a moment." ●

FRANK PACK: A BIBLIOGRAPHY

Compiled by R. L. Roberts, archivist, Center for Restoration Studies, Abilene Christian University, and Steven Martin, senior religion major, Pepperdine University.

I. PUBLISHED WORKS: Books and Pamphlets.
II. PUBLISHED WORKS: Articles in Books.
III. PUBLISHED WORKS: Articles in Periodicals.
Alternative . . . . Altern.
Christian Chronicle CC
Discipliana . . . . Disc.
Exegete . . . . Exeg.
Firm Foundation . . . . FirmF.
Gospel Advocate . . . . GospA.
Image Magazine . . . . Image
Journal of the Evangelical Theological Society . . . . J EvThS.
Mission . . . . Miss.
Power for Today . . . . PfT.
Restoration Quarterly . . . . RestQ.
20th Century Christian . . . . 20thCC.
Upreach . . . . Upreach
Voice of Freedom . . . . V Free.
IV. PUBLISHED WORKS: Book Reviews.
V. UNPUBLISHED WORKS: Lectures, Papers and Reviews.
VI. UNPUBLISHED WORKS: Thesis and Dissertation.
VII. WORKS IN VIDEO.
VIII. WORKS EDITED.

I. PUBLISHED WORKS: Books and Pamphlets.

1940
Lessons in Church History, Tennessee: Cole Printing Co.

1963
Sermons of Frank Pack, Abilene, Texas: Biblical Research Press (Great Preachers of Today, v. 5).

1965
Revelation, Part 1, Chapters 1-11, Austin, Texas: R. B. Sweet Co., Inc.
Revelation, Part 2, Chapters 12-22, Austin, Texas: R. B. Sweet Co., Inc.

1969
Preaching to Modern Man, Co-author with Prentice Meador, Jr., Abilene, Texas: Biblical Research Press.

1972
Tongues and the Holy Spirit, Abilene, Texas: Biblical Research Press (Way of Life Series).

1975
The Gospel according to John: Part I, 1-10:42, Austin, Texas: R. B. Sweet Co., Inc.

1977
The Gospel according to John: Part II, Austin, Texas: R. B. Sweet Co., Inc.

1983
Evangelho Segundo Joao, Portuguese translation of The Gospel according to John, Parts I and II, Sao Paulo, Brazil: Editora Vida Crista.

1984
The Message of the New Testament, The Revelation, Parts I and II, Abilene, Texas: Biblical Research Press.

II. PUBLISHED WORKS: Articles in Books.

1950
"The Church and the Times," in Abilene Christian College Bible Lectures, Austin, Texas: Firm Foundation Publishing House, 79-91.

1954
"Overcoming Problems in Worship," in Abilene Christian College Bible Lectures, Austin, Texas: Firm Foundation Publishing House, 114-129.

1958
"God and Human Suffering," in Abilene Christian College Bible Lectures, Austin, Texas: Firm Foundation Publishing House, 128-142.

1959
"The Mission of the Church: Helping Those in Need," in Harding College Lectureship, Austin, Texas: Firm Foundation Publishing House, 147-162.
"Preparing the Missionary" in Abilene Christian College Bible Lectures, Austin, Texas: Firm Foundation Publishing House, 115-136.

1962
"Blood"; "Script"; "Joy"; "Sergius Paulus"; "Epistles, Spurious";
"Doxologies." Articles in The Wycliffe Bible Encyclopedia, Chicago: Moody Press.
"The Living Word for Living Man," in Harding College Lectureship, Austin, Texas: Firm Foundation Publishing House, 142.
"Romans," in Fort Worth Christian College Lectures, Fort Worth, Texas: FWCC Bookstore, 99-114.

1964
"Reviving Daily Teaching," in Arizona Bible Lectures, 2nd., Phoenix, Arizona: Highway House.

1966
"The Inspiration of the Scripture" in Abilene Christian College Bible Lectures, Abilene Texas: ACU Students Exchange, 30-46.
"Septuagint," in The New Smith's Bible Dictionary, ed. Reuel Lemmons, Garden City: Doubleday & Company, Inc., 346-348.

1967
"The Power of Prayer," in Great Sermons, Austin, Texas: R. B. Sweet & Co., Inc. 142-149.

1968
"The Role of the Christian Journal: The Editor's Responsibilities" in Abilene Christian College Bible Lectures, Abilene, Texas: ACU Bookstore, 466-471.
"The Story of Redemption — New Testament," in My Best Book, Gastonia, N. Carolina, Good Will Publications, Inc. (The Master Library, v10).
"The Story of Redemption — Old Testament," in My Best Book, Gastonia, N. Carolina, Good Will Publications, Inc. (The Master Library, v10).

1971
"The Revelation of God in Christ," in Harding Graduate School of Religion. The Inspiration and Authority of the Bible, Nashville, Tennessee, Gospel Advocate Company, 141-155.

1972
"Acts 17:31: The Final Judgment," in Lubbock Christian College. Lectures, Lubbock, Texas: Lubbock Christian College, 29-37.

1973
"The Inspiration of the Scriptures," in Pillars of Faith, Ed. by H. O. Wilson and Morris M. Womack, Grand Rapids: Baker Book House, 175-185.

1980
"Exegesis of Revelation 20:1-6," in Abilene Christian University Bible Lectures, Abilene, Texas: ACU Bookstore, 153-168.
"First They Gave Themselves," in Harding University Lectures, Austin, Texas: Firm Foundation Publishing House, 367-375.

1984
"Foreword," in Sacredness and Authority of the Bible, by Bill Patterson, Dallas: Gospel Teachers Publications.
"Grace in Galatians," in Harding University Lectures, Delight, Arkansas, Gospel Light Publishing Co., 18-25.

1986
"Textual Criticism," in Biblical Interpretation, Ed. by Furman Kearley, Grand Rapids: Baker Book House.

III. PUBLISHED WORKS: Articles in Periodicals.

1941
"The Synoptic Gospels," GospA. LXXXIII (December 25), 1237.

1949
"Christians Must Be Peacemakers," 20thCC. XI (April), 26.
"Confess Your Faults," 20thCC. XI (July), 3.

1950
"What is Wrong with Gambling," 20thCC. XII (March), 20.
"What is Your Role in This Drama?" 20thCC. XII (June), 3.
"A Comradeship Through Prayer," 20thCC. XII (August), 23.
"Nurture the New Christian," 20thCC. XIII (November), 33.
"Confess Your Faults," 20thCC. XIII (December), 22.

1951

"Modernist Conception of Paul (1)," GospA. XCIII (October 22), 675.
"Modernist Conception of Paul (2)," GospA. XCIII (November 1), 694.
"Modernism Views Jesus (1)," GospA. XCIII (August 9), 502.
"Modernism Views Jesus (2)," GospA. XCIII (September 13), 580.
"Modernism Views Jesus (3)," GospA. XCIII (October 4), 630.
"What is Modernism? (1)," GospA. XCIII (June 28), 402.
"What is Modernism? (2)," GospA. XCIII (July 26), 469.
"Lift Up Your Eyes and Look," 20thCC. XIII (January), 13.
"What is Your Role in This Drama," 20thCC. XIII (June), 3.
"Yield Not to Temptation," 20thCC. XIII (August), 34.
"How the Bible Was Written," 20thCC. XIV (November), 7.

1952

"Archaeological Confirmations of the Bible," GospA. XCIV (December 4), 790.
"The Meaning of Inspiration," GospA. XCIV (December 11), 803.
"The Meaning of Revelation," GospA. XXCIV (November 6), 713.
"Our Father Who Art in Heaven," 20thCC. XIV (March), 20.
"Confession of Faith in Christ," 20thCC. XIV (May), 17.
"Do You Really Worship God?" 20thCC. XIV (June), 16.
"Do You Take Your Vows Seriously?" 20thCC. XV (October), 3.

1953

"Breaking Bread Each Lord's Day," 20thCC. XVI (November), 9.
"The Church and the Alcohol Problem," 20thCC. XV (January), 27.
"The General Texts of Inspiration," GospA. XCV (January 29), 56.
"How Christian Schools Can Help," 20thCC. XV (May), 11.
"Importance of Proper Bible Study," GospA. XCV (September 10), 569.
"The Offense of the Cross," 20thCC. XV (August), 14.
"Qualifications and Requirements of Proper Bible Study," GospA. XCV (September 24), 612.
"Tools of Bible Study: Reference Bibles and Their Use," GospA. XCV (October 8), 655.
"Tools of Bible Study: Bible Dictionaries and Encyclopedias," GospA. XCV (November 5), 732.
"Tools of Bible Study: Bible Geographies and Atlases," GospA. XCV (November 19), 777.
"Tools of Bible Study: Archeology," GospA. XCV (December 3), 812.
"Tools of Bible Study: Hebrew Grammars and Lexicons," GospA. XCV (December 17), 857.

1954

"Confessing our Faults," FirmF. LXXI (September 28), 8.
"Keep the Door of My Lips," GospA. XCVI (September 23), 746.
"The Seven-fold Oneness Christ Desires," 20thCC. XVII (November), 18.
"Tools of Bible Study: Greek Grammars and Lexicons," GospA. XCVI (January 7), 11.
"Tools of Bible Study: Modern Speech Versions of the Bible," GospA. XCVI (February 18), 132.
"Tools of the Bible Study: Commentaries," GospA. XCVI (April 22), 308.
"A Valuable Book," GospA. XCVI (September 16), 729.

1955
"The Bible is Inspired of God," PfT. 1 (October), 39.
"Gospel Advocate Honored at A.C.C. Lectureship," GospA. XCVII (March 17), 209.
"Jesus' Example in Baptism," 20thCC. XVIII (December), 6.
"Ten Million Readers," GospA. XCVII (December 8), 1110.
"Turning Many to God," PfT. 1 (January), 5.
"Was Peter Ever in Rome? The Biblical Evidence," GospA. XCVII (April 28), 321.
"Was Peter Ever in Rome? The Traditional Evidence," GospA. XCVII (May 26), 413.
"Why We Believe the Bible," GospA. XCVII (July 14), 592.
"Understanding Adults," FirmF. LXXII (November 8), 733.

1956
'The Living Christ: My Heart," 20thCC. XIX (December), 22.
"Vacation Time Again," GospA. XCVIII (June 21), 561.
"Windows Opened Toward Jerusalem," GospA. XCVIII (December 6), 953.

1957
"The Canonicity of the Scriptures," GospA. XCIX (February 28), 140.
"Every Teacher Teaching Christ by Precept and Example (1 & 2)," GospA. XCIX (November 14), 726; (December 12), 792. Lecture at Abilene Christian College. Faculty Conference.
"God's Wise Little People," 20thCC. XIX (May), 15.
"The Good News of Rest," PfT. III (May), 13.
"Saved by Grace," GospA. XCIX (July 18), 449.
"Some Modern Views on Infant Baptism," RestQ. I (4th Qr), 220-226.
"This Day Belongs to God," GospA. XCIX (September 5), 562.
"Training the Preacher," GospA. XCIX (May 2), 279.
"What Do Ye More Than Others?" GospA. XCIX (August 8), 497.
"What is Faith?" 20thCC. XX (December), 5.

1958
"Can an Educated Person Believe in the Virgin Birth?" 20thCC. XXI (December), 28.
"My Stewardship of Talent," 20thCC. XX (June), 6.
"Spiritual Food for the Soul," GospA. C (October 30), 693.
"The Power of God's Word," GospA. C (November 20), 738.
"Thy Word is a Lamp unto My Feet," GospA. C (October 2), 625.
"Worship: What is It?" 20thCC. XX (February), 21.

1959
"Does I Corinthians 15:23-24 Teach a Premillennial Reign of Christ on Earth?" RestQ. III (4th Qr), 205-213).
"Faith and Works," 20thCC. XXI (August), 14.
"God's Fruitful Word," GospA. CI (July 23), 468.
"One Hundred Years Ago: 1859," GospA. CI (November 19), 737.
"The Power of God's Word," GospA. CI (June 11), 370.
"Amendment 18: The 25th Anniversary of Repeal," 20th CC. XXI (February), 11.
"Who Sets the Standards?" 20th CC. XXII (October), 3.
"Why Couldn't This Happen Among Us?" GospA. CI (November 5), 705.

1960
"Cultivate the Fine Art of Good Cheer," 20th CC. XXIII (November), 28.
"God and His People: The Potter and the Clay," GospA. CII (November 24), 746.
"How to Enter the Church," GospA. CII (March 24), 185.
"Origen's Evaluation of Textual Variants in the Greek Bible," RestQ. IV (3rd Qr), 139-146.
"The Sheep of His Pasture," GospA. CII (December 1), 759.
"A Study of Papyrus Bodmer II (P66)," RestQ. IV (1st Qr), 1-10; (2nd Qr), 61-70.
"The Western Text of Acts," RestQ. IV (4th Qr), 220-234.

1961
"The Contribution of Textual Criticism to the Interpretation of the New Testament," RestQ. V (4th Qr), 179-192.
"The Father's Love for His Son," GospA. CIII (January 5), 2.
"God and His People: The Vineyard," GospA. CIII (May 4), 277.
"Peace, Be Still," 20thCC. XXIV (November), 16.
"Respect of Persons," 20thCC. XXIII (April), 14.
"What is Covetousness?" PfT. V (September 1), 2.
"The Word 'Church,'" GospA. CIII (December 14), 785.

1962
"The Church as Jesus Saw It," GospA. CIV (January 4), 4.
"I Will Build My Church," GospA. CIV (October 4), 631.
"Jesus and the Kingdom," GospA. CIV (July 12), 433.
"A Modern Challenge," 20thCC. XXIV (February), 12.
"The Nature of the Kingdom in Jesus' Teaching," GospA. CIV (September 13), 586.
"Our Leadership is Coming," 20thCC. XXV (October), 59.
"The Significance of Vatican Council II," GospA. CIV (September 6), 568.

1963
"God Speaks Through His Son: The Supreme Revelation," 20thCC. XXV (September), 17.
"The Gospel of John in the Twentieth Century," RestQ. VII (4th Qr), 173-185.
"An Interesting Textual Study of Second Timothy," GospA. CV (September 5), 564.
"The Resurrection in Early Preaching," 20thCC. XXV (April), 8.
"Soldiers of Courage," GospA. CV (November 7), 705.
"What Does Worship Mean to You?" GospA. CV (May 16), 306.

1964
"Difficult Places," GospA. CVI (June 25), 401.
"God is the Audience," 20thCC. XXVII (November), 31.
"He is Coming Again," 20thCC. XXVI (July), 22.
"Soldiers of Courage," FirmF. LXXXI (January 7), 8.
"That We May Serve More," GospA. CVI (November 19), 740.
"Worship in Spirit and in Truth," FirmF. LXXXI (April 21), 245.

1965
"Biblical Standards of Morality," 20thCC. XXVII (January), 28.
"The Central Purpose of Life," GospA. CVII (April 15), 237.

"Our Light Afflictions," 20thCC. XXVII (March), 16.
"Our Most Important Outside Reading — The Bible," 20thCC. XXVII (August), 9.
"Three Christian Educators Honored," GospA. CVII (July 15), 449.

1966
"An Evaluation of the Revised Standard Version, Catholic Edition," RestQ. IX (1st Qr), 21-30.
"The Holy Spirit: Who or What?" 20thCC. XXIX (November), 5.
"The Passing of Three Great Men," GospA. CVIII (January 13), 18.
"To a Great Elder," GospA. CVIII (November 10), 714.
"Twenty-five Years of Teaching in Christian Colleges," GospA. CVIII (March 17), 169.

1967
"Discipleship on the Campus," Miss. I (August), 47.
"Over A Century of Service," GospA. CIX (June 15), 373.
"Take and Read," PfT. III (May), 5.

1968
"Another Elder Honored," GospA. CX (February 15), 99.
"Shall We Glorify Violence?" 20thCC. XXX (September), 16.
"Some Reassuring Experiences," FirmF. XVC (November 5), 712.
Ibid., GospA. CX (October 24), 677.

1969
"The Christ of the Gospels? A Response," Miss. II (April), 13.
"How Do We Know the Bible is Inspired?" GospA. CXI (January 23), 61.
"Teaching the Bible and Religion at Pepperdine," FirmF. LXXXV (October 28), 678.
"We Pray with the Psalmist," PfT. XV (January), 29.

1970
"The Early Church Shows and Shares the Living Christ," 20thCC. XXXII (April), 35.
"God's Call to Change," GospA. CXII (October 15), 668.
"In Memory of a Dear Friend and Brother," GospA. CXII (January 15), 40.
"Work and Word," GospA. CXII (March 5), 155.

1971
"Some Great Things Are Happening," FirmF. LXXXVII (November 2), 695.
"Ibid., GospA. CXIII (November 18), 725.

1973
"I Met a Man," PfT. XIX (October), 53.
"Problems in the Translation of the Gospel of John," RestQ. XVI (3rd & 4th Qr), 209-218.
"Repent and Be Converted," 20thCC. XXXV (March), 16.
"Worship," 20thCC. XXXVI (October), 22.
1974
"Build on Jesus," PfT. XX (April), 50.
"Radiant Faith and Courage," Co-author with Della Pack, 20thCC. XXXVI (August), 9.

1975
"Glenn L. Wallace Honored," GospA. CXVII (November 27), 756.
"Has Your Life Style Changed?" PfT. XXI (September), 33.
"What is Faith?" 20thCC. XXXVII (July), 24.

1976
"Boasting in the Lord," RestQ. XIX (2nd Qr), 65-71.
"Gus Nichols, A Great Man of God," GospA. XCIII (March 25), 199.
"Pentecostalism and Neo-Pentecostalism," Altern. II (April), 1.

1977
"The Lord's Supper," PfT. XXIII (February), 39.
"The New Birth," PfT. XXIII (January), 11.

1978
"Mysticism — Why Its Appeal?" GospA. CXX (March 2), 129.

1979
"Baptism and Faith," 20thCC. XLI (June), 9.
"The Lord Weighs the Heart," 20thCC. XLI (April), 20.
"Recent Celebrations," GospA. CXXI (March 22), 183.
"Study of Romans 8:28," RestQ. XXII (1st & 2nd Qr), 44-53.
"Federal Court Declares Transcendental Meditation a Religion," FirmF. XCVI (October 23), 682.
"Understanding Inspiration," Upreach I (August), 18.
"An Unprecedented Accomplishment," FirmF. XCVI (May 22), 323.

1980
"The Case for Congregational Singing," 20thCC. XLII (September), 18.
"Hannah, The Prayerful Mother," 20thCC. XLII (January), 29
"Triumphal Procession in Christ," GospA. CXXXII (July 10), 401.

1981
"Biblical Word Study: Basileia: 'Kingdom'," Exeg. I (September), 1.
"Faith and Works," PfT. XXVII (November), 41.
"Watch and Pray," PfT. XXVII (September), 80.

1982
"Celebration of Heritage Observed," FirmF. IC (March 2), 131.
"Justified (Saved) by Faith," 20thCC. XLIV (February), 24.

1983
"Amos Lincoln Cassius: Pioneer Black Leader," Disc. XLIII (Summer), 25.
"Biblical Word Study: Logos: 'Word'," Exeg. II (June), 1.
"Drawn to God," GospA. CXXV (October 20), 516.
"One Hundred Years Since Westcott and Hort," RestQ. XXVI (2nd Qr), 65-79.
"She Hath Done What She Could," 20thCC. XLVC (September), 23.

1985
"Jesus Came Preaching," V Free. XXXIII (June), 87.
"Historical Perspectives — Part I," Image, I (November 15), 16-17.
"Historical Perspectives — Part II," Image, I (December 15), 10-13.

1986
"Man's Sinfulness and God's Righteousness," 20th CC, XLVI (February), 4-6.

IV. PUBLISHED WORKS: Book Reviews.

1957

Bruce, F. F., The Acts of the Apostles, RestQ. 1 (3rd Qr), 144.
Bruce, F. F., Commentary on the Book of Acts, RestQ. I (3rd Qr), 143.
Gaster, Theodor Herzl, The Dead Sea Scrolls in English Translation, RestQ. I (3rd Qr), 142.

1962

Bales, James D., Communism: Its Faith and Fallacies, RestQ. VI (3rd Qr), 105-106.
"The Interpreter's Dictionary of the Bible," RestQ. VI (3rd Qr), 151-155.

1963

"Books to Challenge Christian Thinking," 20thCC. XXV (February), 27.
"Books to Challenge Christian Thinking," 20thCC. XXV (May), 13.

1969

Tillich, Paul, Perspectives on 19th and 20th Century Protestant Theology, RestQ. XII (1st Qr), 55-56.

1973

Warren, Thomas B., Have Atheists Proved There is No God? GospA. CXIII (February, 8), 86.

1981

Feinberg, Charles L., Millennialism: The Two Major Views, J EvThS. XXIV (December), 343-344.

V. UNPUBLISHED WORKS: Lectures, Papers, and Reviews.

1964

"Philosophical and Ideological Factors in our Environment Endangering Faith and Exerting Pressure on Us to Compromise Principle," San Diego, California, Teacher Training School.
"The Gospel of John in the Twentieth Century," Pepperdine College. Bible Forum.

1965

"Finding Tomorrow's Leaders," Church of Christ, San Leandro, California, Lectureship Workshop, January 29-30.
"The Holy Spirit," Pepperdine College Lectureship.
"The Prayer of Sonship"; "Heart Guardianship"; "The Love-badge of Discipleship"; "Better Churches Through Involvement"; "Better Churches Through Inspiration"; "Better Churches Through Instruction." Columbia Christian College Lectureship, September 22-24.

1966

"Inspiration of the Scriptures," Abilene Christian College Lectureship. Biblical Forum.

1967

"Leadership in Church Planning: Benevolence; Planning and Supervising a Mission Program; Planning a Church Budget; and Church Discipline." Mid-South Training Series, 8th, Memphis, Tennessee, March 27-30.

"The Crisis in Preaching Today; Laying the Foundation; Confronting Our Audience; One Man's Way of Working; Why I Preach; Where the Action Is; A Seeking Ministry; The Faith We Preach." Abilene Christian College, Lectures on Preaching, 17th, October 2-5.

1968
"Religious Authority," Oklahoma Christian College Lectureship, Main Lecture.
"Preacher's Book Review Class," Abilene Christian College Bible Lectures.

1969
"The Christian in the Community," Christian College of the Southwest Lectureship, Dallas, Texas.
"A Great Challenge and Sectarianism in the Church," Freed-Hardeman College Lectures.
"The Sin of Racism," Pepperdine College Lectureship.
"Commission," Panel Discussion, Abilene Christian College Bible Lectures.

1970
"The Library of Higher Education," Friends of the Library Lecture. Abilene Christian College Bible Lectures.

1971
"The Question of Tongues Today," Abilene Christian College. Preacher's Workshop.

1972
"Problems in the Translation of the Gospel of John," Abilene Christian College. Biblical Forum.

1973
"Cessation of the Miraculous Gifts," Abilene Christian College. Preacher's Workshop.

1974
"Purity," Main Lecture. Lubbock Christian College Lectureship.

1975
"Millennium Optimism Today: Fantasy or Reality," Harding Graduate School of Religion. Fall Workshop, September 15-16.
"Boasting in the Lord," Abilene Christian College. Bible Forum.
"Baptism and the New Life," Main Lecture. Pepperdine University Lectureship.

1976
"Our Real Purpose: Philippians 3:14-25," Pepperdine University Lectureship.

1978
"That the Leadership May be Edified," San Diego, CA. Lectureship, El Cajon Church of Christ.

1979
"Identifying the Falling Away: A Historical Study," Abilene Christian University. Bible Forum.
"Reaching Modern Man with a Personal God," Main Lecture. Oklahoma Christian College Lectureship.
"Introduction to Biblical Inspiration"; "Biblical Inerrancy"; "Biblical Interpretation"; "Biblical Interpretation and Authority." Great Lakes Christian College Lectureship, Beamsville, Ontario, May 28-30.

"New Testament Spirituality," Whippany, New Jersey. Church of Christ. Workshop.
"The Holy Spirit," Workshop. Syracuse, New York.

1980
"Working with Our Wives"; "Working Together in Promoting the Gospel"; Shenandoah, California, Preachers'/Wives' Retreat.
"Stewards of the Word," Harding University Lectureship. Preachers and Elders Dinner.
"A Time for Pure Religion: James 1:27," Main Lecture, Pepperdine University Lectureship.

1981
"The Living God," Pepperdine University Lectureship.
Review of: Packer, James I., Beyond the Battle for the Bible, Staley Lectures, Pepperdine University.

1982
"Does God Exist?" San Gabriel, California, Seminar, October 15-17.
"Food That Perishes, Food That Endures: John 6:26-58," Main Lecture. Pepperdine University Lectureship.
"Ministry 1930-1970 in Our Movement," Abilene Christian University. Christian Scholars' Conference.
Review of: Kidner, Derek, A Time to Mourn and a Time to Dance, Preacher's Luncheon, Pepperdine University.
Review of: Woodroof, James S., Beyond Crossroads, Preacher' Luncheon, Pepperdine University.

1983
"The Prologue: The Word Became Flesh"; "Discipleship and the Word"; "Washing the Diciples' Feet"; "The Lordship of Jesus." Oklahoma Christian College. Faculty Conference Bible Study.
"The Washing of Rebirth," Pepperdine University Lectureship. Issues Forum.

1984
"Historical Perspectives," Restoration Forum Three, Pepperdine University.
"Response to 'Women and Ministry' by Phil Ware," Abilene Christian University, Christian Scholars' Conference.
Review of: McMillon, Lynn, Restoration Roots. CC, XLI (May), 15.

1986
"Man of Sorrows — What a Name", main Lecture, Pepperdine University Lectureship.

VI. UNPUBLISHED WORKS: Thesis and Dissertation.

1939
"The Dependent Child in Tennessee," M.A. Thesis, Vanderbilt University. 1948
"The Methodology of Origen as a Textual Critic in Arriving at the Text of the New Testament," Ph.D. Dissertation, University of Southern California.

VII. WORKS IN VIDEO.

1982
"The Gospel of John," West Monroe, Louisiana, International Video Bible Lessons. Twenty-six Videotape Cassettes.

VIII. WORKS EDITED.

1953
Abilene Christian College. Our Bible. Ed. by Frank Pack, Abilene, Texas: Abilene Christian College.

1962
Roberson, Charles Heber, "The Meaning and the Use of Psallo," RestQ. VI (1st Qr), 19-31; (2nd Qr), 57-66. Ed. by Frank Pack and J. W. Roberts.

Ruby Green, the widow of Dr. William M. Green, stands with four of the first five lecturers in the William M. Green Lecture Series at Pepperdine. From left to right, the lecturers are John F. Wilson, Carl Mitchell, J.P. Sanders, and Frank Pack. W.B. West, Jr. could not be present for the photo which was taken at the Green Lecture Program in October, 1984.

A familiar scene - Frank Pack at the Pepperdine Lectures in 1985.